AS OTHERS SEE US

AS OTHERS SEE US

The Causes and Consequences of
Foreign Perceptions of America

STEPHEN BROOKS

broadview press

LIBRARY AND ARCHIVES CANADA CATALOGUING IN PUBLICATION

Brooks, Stephen, 1956–
    As others see us : the causes and consequences of foreign perceptions of America / Stephen Brooks.

Includes bibliographical references and index.
ISBN 1-55111-688-X

1. United States—Civilization—1970–. 2. National characteristics, American.
3. United States—Foreign relations—2001–. 4. United States—Foreign public opinion.
5. Anti-Americanism. I. Title.

E169.12.B727 2006   973.931   C2006-900043-3

BROADVIEW PRESS, LTD. is an independent, international publishing house, incorporated in 1985. Broadview believes in shared ownership, both with its employees and with the general public; since the year 2000 Broadview shares have traded publicly on the Toronto Venture Exchange under the symbol BDP.

We welcome comments and suggestions regarding any aspect of our publications—please feel free to contact us at the addresses below or at broadview@broadviewpress.com/www.broadviewpress.com.

North America
Post Office Box 1243,
Peterborough, Ontario, Canada K9J 7H5

Post Office Box 1015,
3576 California Road,
Orchard Park, New York, USA 14127
TEL: (705) 743-8990; FAX: (705) 743-8353

customerservice@broadviewpress.com

UK, Ireland and continental Europe
Plymbridge Distributors Ltd.
Estover Road, Plymouth PL6 7PY, UK
TEL: 44 (0) 1752 202301;
FAX ORDER LINE: 44 (0) 1752 202333;
ORDERS: orders@nbnplymbridge.com
CUST. SERV.: cservs@nbnplymbridge.com

Australia and New Zealand
UNIREPS University of New South Wales
Sydney, NSW 2052 Australia
TEL: 61 2 96640999; FAX: 61 2 96645420
infopress@unsw.edu.au

Broadview Press gratefully acknowledges the financial support of the Government of Canada through the Book Publishing Industry Development Program for our publishing activities.

Interior by Liz Broes, Black Eye Design.
Cover by Matthew Jubb, Black Eye Design.

The author of the book and the publisher have made every attempt to locate authors of copyrighted material or their heirs and assigns, and would be grateful for information that would allow them to correct any errors or omissions in a subsequent edition of the work.

Printed in Canada
10 9 8 7 6 5 4 3 2 1

Contents

List of Illustrations

PLATES

Preface

The idea for this book began germinating over a decade ago when I spent a year teaching in Belgium, at the Katholieke Universiteit Leuven and Vesalius College. I wanted the experience of teaching abroad, and so I proposed to these two institutions a list of courses that I felt competent to teach. The answer I got back from both was the same: They wanted me to teach American politics. And despite the fact that English was not the first language of any of my students at Leuven and of only a handful at Vesalius, my classes were full. Not only were the classrooms full, the students were also enthusiastic and even fairly knowledgeable about the United States. Many of them had visited, of course, but all had ideas, images, and opinions about America. It was then that I understood in an immediate way the import of "America the beguiling," a phrase that I would come across several years later (Joffe, 2001).

A number of years passed, however, before I started to write and teach about foreign perspectives on America, starting with a senior seminar that I offered at the University of Michigan in 2000 and my book *America through Foreign Eyes: Classic Interpretations of American Political Life* (2002). I had just finished writing that book when the tragic events of 9/11 rocked America and the world. Suddenly, my research and teaching interests moved from the respectable margins to the center of the public conversation. Americans who were not in the habit of wondering what the world thought of them or why would ask these questions with a vengeance over the subsequent years. Instant analyses of a superficial sort or motivated by a political agenda sprang up alongside more thoughtful examinations. The war in Iraq merely served to sharpen Americans' awareness of the world's gaze.

11

I wanted to write a book that would provide an understanding—one rooted in history and empirical data—of how Americans have been understood by other populations and challenge what I believe to be the facile conventional wisdom on anti-Americanism. A chance encounter in Portland, Oregon, with Michael Harrison, publisher of Broadview Press, provided me with the opportunity. Michael had acquired two of my earliest books in the 1980s, when he was college editor with McClelland & Stewart. He liked the idea of this book, and so we resumed a professional relationship that had begun two decades ago. I hope readers will judge that Michael's faith in my project was not misplaced.

I have had many copy editors for many books over the years, but never one more meticulous in her reading of the manuscript or more thoughtful in her suggestions than Catherine Dorton. It was a pleasure to work with her. Greg Yantz, who joined Broadview while I was working on this book, was supportive at every stage. Lorraine Cantin and Luc Quenville of Document Services at the University of Windsor were indispensable in helping me transform data into reader friendly charts and tables. And I would be remiss if I failed to mention my students at the University of Michigan and the University of Windsor. They were my sounding board for the arguments and analyses presented in this book. Their reactions and presentations influenced my thinking about these matters.

Finally, as always, I would like to thank my family for what doubtless seemed to be my occasional distraction, stealing time from its rightful owners.

Stephen Brooks
Ann Arbor and Windsor

Introduction

"Why do they hate us?" Seldom posed before September 11, 2001, this question came to preoccupy Americans in the aftermath of the terrorist attacks on that day. A range of answers were given, from President George W. Bush's assessment that the terrorists hated the values and freedoms embodied by America, to social critic Noam Chomsky's argument that the attacks were a response to exploitation and injustice experienced abroad, perpetrated and abetted by American policies, governments, and interests. In true American fashion, opportunity was seized and a small industry arose from the ashes of the World Trade Center—an industry of self-analysis and national introspection such as had never been seen in the history of the republic. Changing planes at George Bush Intercontinental Airport in Houston two months after the attacks, I passed the time leafing through the pages of several books in a genre that scarcely existed before 9/11, a genre whose defining pillars are "who are they?" and "why do they hate us?"

From these small beginnings, a mountain of print and electronic reflection has developed, in both the United States and many other countries. The triumphalism that characterized the American colossus during much of the previous decade—inspired by the collapse of Soviet Communism, the embrace of market reforms in China, and the apparent victory of capitalist democracy throughout an increasing share of the world, under the unchallenged leadership of the United States—was generally untouched by curiosity about the world's opinion. Evidence of vulnerability at home changed that. In the 2000 primary campaigns, candidate Bush appeared confused by a reporter's question about the Taliban, seeming not to recognize the word. Less than two years later, President Bush experienced no such confusion. Indifference and a lack of curiosity clearly were no longer options.

Americans and their leaders are, on the whole, much more aware today that what the world outside their borders thinks does in fact matter. The attacks of September 11, 2001—celebrated in some parts of the world and sympathized with in others—were the wake-up call. Subsequent events reinforced Americans' dawning awareness that their country is not always loved abroad, for example, German, French, and Russian resistance to the Bush administration's plans for regime change in Saddam Hussein's Iraq in 2003; the unprecedented size of demonstrations in opposition to a war in Iraq throughout much of the world; foreign criticism of US failure to ratify either the Kyoto Accord or the international treaty banning landmines or to join the International Criminal Court; and the hailstorm of censure on issues ranging from trade, genetically modified organisms, and capital punishment, which has been eliminated in virtually all other Western democracies.

But while the world's view is not always favorable, it is not always negative or hostile either. This simple fact is often in danger of being overlooked in all the angst and analysis of hostility toward America, hostility that undeniably exists now in many parts of the world and has also existed in the past. One of the principal arguments of this book is that the phenomenon of anti-Americanism—its nature, extent, and origin—is very poorly understood, often grossly exaggerated, and frequently attributed to the wrong causes. In order to understand world opinion, it is necessary to examine what and how foreign populations learn about the United States, including America's culture, politics, economy, and the motives behind and consequences of its actions abroad.

Two important findings emerge from such an examination. First, it is frequently a mistake to locate the causes of foreign sentiment toward the United States primarily in the policies of American governments and the behavior of those who represent America and project its image overseas. Perceptions of the United States and its people are only partly based on US actions and the reality of the American experience. Often they are based as much or more on characteristics of the beholder. It follows that the United States cannot wholly remedy its "image problem" through its own actions.

Second, the question of how others see America should not be treated in isolation from that of how Americans view the world outside their own borders. The events of September 11, 2001, brought the world to America's cognitive doorstep in an unprecedented way, even more traumatically than the 1941 attack on Pearl Harbor.

Everyone has agreed that ignorance, indifference, and isolationism no longer appear to be options. But making all Americans—not just the small fraction who pay serious attention to the world outside their borders—aware of and sensitive to foreign perceptions of the United States is no simple task. The cognitive isolationism of Americans and the media system most of them rely on runs deep.

Not only do most Americans pay little attention to most of the world most of the time, their ability to understand other people and societies is also impeded by a wall of incomprehension that separates America from even those societies whose standard of living and institutions are broadly similar to their own. But this is a two-way street. While Americans often fail to understand the positions, sentiments, and values of others, these other populations also fail to understand those of Americans. The gap that separates the values and beliefs of Americans from those of the French, the Germans, and the Spanish, for example, is a factor that influences how America is viewed by people in these other countries.

One of the ironies of a post-cold war world in which the power of the United States is without rival is that the costs of isolationism and ignorance are greater than ever before. At the same time, however, the temptation to imagine that the rest of the world mattered less than before was never greater, as America briefly basked in the triumphant glow of a world in which capitalism and democracy, under the aegis of American leadership, were thought to have vanquished all rivals. Although it is unlikely that Americans will come to pay much attention to the rest of the world any time soon—except when their citizens are shot at, blown up, or kidnapped and beheaded abroad, or when they are persuaded that the threat of foreigners doing harm to them at home seems real—their failure to do so cripples their ability to understand a world in which American interests, security, and prosperity are dependent to an unprecedented degree.

My investigation of the causes and consequences of the world's perceptions of America is built upon a simple and undeniable premise that is too often ignored or discounted as unimportant. This premise is that the images and ideas foreign populations have of the United States and Americans come from a number of information sources, most of which are mediated. By this I mean that foreign perceptions are not acquired firsthand, but rely instead on secondary accounts. Some of these sources are American: Hollywood, for example, is a major source of images and ideas about the

United States consumed outside the country. Other sources originate outside the United States, in the media, educational, religious, and political systems that teach foreign populations about America. Any attempt to understand the *what* and *why* of foreign perceptions needs to look closely at these external determinants of how the images and interpretations of America are constructed in different societies.

What I would characterize as the conventional wisdom on why foreign populations view America as they do tends to emphasize what America *does* rather than what it is *seen to be*. I do not argue that the actions of Americans, their governments, their corporations, or any other emissaries—official or unofficial—are inconsequential to understanding foreign perceptions. But I do think that the balance of explanation has for many years leaned too heavily on American actions as the cause of these perceptions. This tendency has been expressed most egregiously and misleadingly in books like Ziauddin Sardar and Merryl Wyn Davies's 2002 bestseller *Why Do People Hate America?* Such analyses are too narrow in their explanation, when they are not downright political in intent. I do not for a moment deny that the actions of Americans and the policies of United States governments have influenced how foreigners view America. But to imagine that these judgments are arrived at independent of the meanings that others ascribe to America—their understanding of what America *is*—is quite naïve and incorrect. It is a mistake that the great foreign interpreters of America in the past, including Alexis de Tocqueville, James Bryce, and Harold Laski, never made. Is there any reason why we should fall prey to it now?

CHAPTER ONE

The THREE "I's" *of* COGNITIVE ISOLATIONISM

All students of American foreign policy know that isolationist impulses have occupied an important place in the minds of Americans ever since George Washington's farewell address of 1800, when he warned his successors and countrymen to beware of "foreign entanglements." These impulses have occasionally had the upper hand over internationalist tendencies in American foreign policy and public opinion, as was true between the First and Second World Wars and, to a much lesser degree and in a very different global environment, after the Vietnam War. Today it is apparent that isolationism is not an option. Indeed, the real debate has long since moved beyond comparing isolationism and internationalism; it now focuses on examining the relative merits of multilateralism in foreign policy versus some form of US-dominated strategy for engaging the world (not to be confused with unilateralism, although this is the label often attached to it by its critics).

Isolationism lives on, however, in one rather important form. It continues to characterize the mind-set of many Americans and even some influential segments of the opinion-leading class in the United States. It is characterized by the three "I's": ignorance, insularity, and indifference. Moreover, the consequences of isolationism for Americans and their understanding of how other national populations perceive them—or as they and their leaders often believe, *mis*perceive them—are undeniable.

IGNORANCE

When Alexis de Tocqueville visited the United States in the 1830s, comparatively few Americans had more than an elementary school education. Nevertheless, Tocqueville was struck by what seemed to him the general level of learning and knowledge among average people. Today, most Americans graduate from high school and about one-quarter of the population has at least some post-secondary education. Notwithstanding that a much greater proportion of the population spends many more years in school than during Tocqueville's time, there can be little doubt that France's greatest interpreter of America would be unimpressed by the level of knowledge characteristic of today's "average American."

Nowhere is the problem of weak and shaky knowledge more evident than in geography. According to the National Geographic-Roper 2002 Global Geographic Literacy Survey of younger adults (ages 18 to 34), Americans are not much different from other national populations in the importance they attach to knowing where countries in the news are located: about 75 per cent responded that this information is either "necessary" or "important." However, the percentage of Americans who believe it to be "absolutely necessary" has declined significantly in recent years (between 1988 and 2002), from 35 per cent to 25 per cent among 18- to 24-year-olds and from 36 per cent to 28 per cent among 25- to 34-year-olds. Younger American adults also believe that their knowledge of geography is as good as or better than that of their foreign counterparts, about 60 per cent agreeing that, in general, Americans know the same amount or more about geography than do the citizens of other countries.

Alas, the reality is rather different. Based on a 56-question quiz that tested respondents' knowledge of current events, international issues, map-reading skills, and world geography, Americans placed second-last among the ten countries surveyed. Mexico brought up the rear. As figure 1.1 shows, the average scores of Americans were not sharply worse than those of Canadians and Britons, but were far below all of the other advanced industrialized democracies included in the study.

When identifying where particular countries are located, younger adult Americans displayed a very shaky grasp of the world's political geography. Their knowledge was particularly weak when it came to Europe, the Middle East, and Asia. American respondents came in dead last, behind

FIGURE 1.1   World Geography Survey (average number of correct answers, by country)

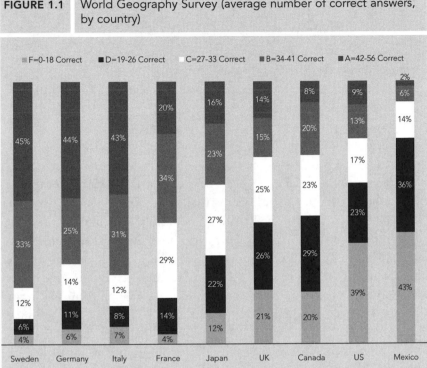

Source: Adapted from National Geographic-Roper 2002 Global Geographic Literacy Survey (November), 17.

Mexicans, in identifying 15 countries and the Pacific Ocean on a map of the world (see figure 1.2). Shockingly, only about one-fifth could correctly locate Egypt (26 per cent), Germany (19 per cent), and Israel (21 per cent).

The news just gets worse. Here are some of the "lowlights" to emerge from the National Geographic's survey of knowledge related to world issues and current events:

- Americans are much less likely than the young adults from all of the other countries surveyed to have a reasonably accurate idea of the size of the United States' population.
- Fewer Americans than any of the other national populations could name Afghanistan, from a list of countries, as the home of the Taliban and the base for al Qaeda—and this was after 9/11 and the invasion of Afghanistan!

- Two-thirds of Americans could identify Cuba, from a list of four countries, as the western hemisphere's only Communist country, but respondents in Italy (91 per cent), Germany (80 per cent), Mexico (80 per cent), Sweden (80 per cent), Canada (73 per cent) and France (72 per cent) were more likely to know.
- Fewer than half of Americans could identify the European Union (EU), from a list of five, as the organization endorsing the euro for its members, compared to virtually all the Europeans surveyed and large majorities among the Japanese, Canadians, and even Mexicans.

Ignorance of this magnitude might be overlooked were it not for the fact that the population it characterizes is that of the world's only superpower whose international reach—militarily, economically, and culturally—far surpasses that of any other country. However, the National Geographic cross-national survey that collected these dismal findings only looked at younger adults, ages 18 to 34. Just as those toward the older end of this age cohort had marginally better knowledge of world geography and current affairs than the younger ones, middle-aged and older Americans are even more knowledgeable. The "60 Minutes" generation (the average viewer of this long-running CBS news and current affairs program is in his or her late fifties) is pretty well-informed about these matters. Moreover, formal education makes a difference in the United States, as it does elsewhere. The National Geographic survey found that those Americans with at least some college education knew much more than those with only high school graduation or less, but still less than the average Swedish, German, Italian, French, or Japanese young adult with less education.

The Pew Center for the People and the Press's Biennial News Consumption Survey in 2002 corroborates the impact of age and education on knowledge about the world. It found that almost twice as many respondents aged 50 to 64 correctly identified Yasser Arafat as head of the PLO compared to those aged 18 to 29 years (60 per cent versus 32 per cent), and they were also far more likely to be able to identify the euro as the new currency of the European Union (55 per cent versus 37 per cent). It is not quite correct, therefore, to say that Americans are woefully ignorant of the world outside their borders. The truth is that being older, male, more educated, born overseas or at least claiming foreign ancestry, and having

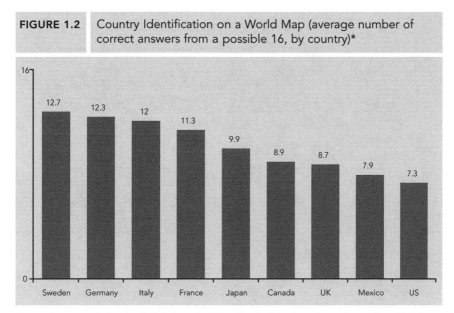

FIGURE 1.2 Country Identification on a World Map (average number of correct answers from a possible 16, by country)*

* Respondents were asked to identify Afghanistan, Argentina, Canada, Cuba, Egypt, France, Germany, Israel, Italy, Japan, Mexico, Pacific Ocean, Russia, Sweden, the UK, and the US.

Source: Adapted from National Geographic-Roper 2002 Global Geographic Literacy Survey (November), 23.

traveled abroad all correlate with significantly greater levels of knowledge of the international scene (Pew 2002b, 23–24).

But no matter how the data is sliced and dissected, the picture that it paints of the general population is both discouraging and worrisome. With these results, who can be surprised that many Americans are genuinely unable to comprehend what appears to be the antipathy that much of the world feels toward them? Ignorance of the world outside their own country is the soil in which this failure grows.

INSULARITY

Part of the explanation for the lamentable ignorance that much of the American population has about the rest of the world, including those regions that are crucially important for US foreign policy, lies in the comparative insularity of their lives. Americans are considerably less likely than those in other affluent democracies to travel outside their own country. They are also less likely than those in other countries, with the exception of

FIGURE 1.3 Foreign Travel Experience in the Past Three Years*

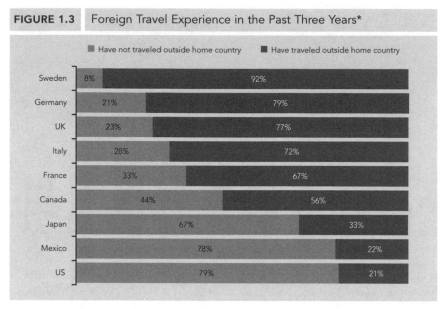

* A small percentage of respondents answered "Don't know," and these figures are not shown.

Totals may not add to 100% because of rounding.

Source: Adapted from National Geographic-Roper 2002 Global Geographic Literacy Survey (November), 40.

FIGURE 1.4 Importance of Speaking a Foreign Language (per cent who agree that it is necessary or important)

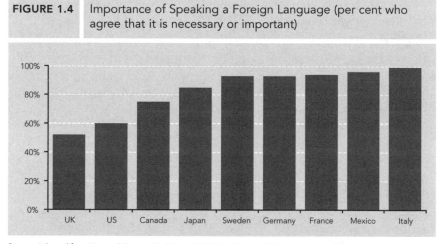

Source: Adapted from National Geographic-Roper 2002 Global Geographic Literacy Survey (November), 13.

Great Britain, to believe that knowing another language is necessary or at least important in today's world.

Two observations are in order. First, the United States is a very large country, both physically and in terms of population, whose only neighboring countries are Canada and Mexico. Foreign travel to countries beyond these two places generally involves taking a plane. (Japan is similarly isolated by geography.) Thus, direct comparisons to smaller countries within comparatively easy distance of each other, as in Europe, may not be fair. Second, a more finely hued analysis of travel would certainly show that more educated and affluent Americans—these attributes are strongly correlated—are considerably more likely than other Americans to have traveled abroad. Moreover, many colleges and universities in the United States have a second-language requirement, and so the more educated strata of the American population is almost certainly more likely than its less educated fellow citizens to believe that knowledge of a foreign language is important.

Nevertheless, the United States stands out as a society where people are less likely to travel abroad and more likely to believe that knowing only one's own language is just fine. Of course, given the global dominance of American English in trade, technology, and science, and its major impact on foreign cultures, Americans' belief in the relative unimportance of other languages is at least understandable from some practical points of view. It may be a liability, however, from the standpoint of understanding other cultures and national perspectives.

Another dimension to American insularity, described by the French philosopher Jean Baudrillard, involves the naïve—in the sense of unreflective and even unconsciousness—belief Americans hold that their society is the fulfillment and embodiment of everything that reasonable people anywhere could aspire to. Baudrillard puts it this way:

> The Americans are not wrong in their idyllic conviction that they are at the center of the world, the supreme power, the absolute model for everyone. And this conviction is not so much founded on natural resources, technologies, and arms, as on the miraculous premise of utopia made reality, of a society which, with a directness we might judge unbearable, is built on the idea that it is the realization of everything the others have dreamt of—justice, plenty, rule of law, wealth,

freedom: it knows this, it believes in it, and in the end, the others have come to believe in it too. (Baudrillard 1988, 77)

What Baudrillard is describing is a philosophical insularity that simply assumes the normality of what might be described as the American model. He does not say that he likes the sort of social and political relations or the culture that is associated with this model. Indeed, it would be hard to find characterizations of America that are bleaker in a postmodern way than Baudrillard's description of New York: "It is a world completely rotten with wealth, power, senility, indifference, Puritanism and mental hygiene, poverty and waste, technological futility, and aimless violence, and yet I cannot help but feel it has about it something of the dawning of the universe" (Baudrillard 1988, 23).

But, like it or not, America is, according to Baudrillard, the authentic form of modernity. When he says that it is "the land of the 'just as it is,'" Baudrillard expresses what he believes to be the naïve, confident, and self-referential mentality of Americans. Interestingly, Baudrillard made this observation about the American spirit many years before Nike adopted "Just Do It" as a marketing slogan. That slogan expresses the same message of confident individualism, unfettered by doubt and fearless of limits. Limits are about the past, about what has been done before, by others, perhaps elsewhere. They are alien to a spirit whose gaze is set on the future and change, on more and better, and whose benchmarks are its own accomplishments, not those of others. The so-called baseball "World Series," the NBA "world" champions, the winner of the Super Bowl as the best football team in the world, the world's *biggest* this, *fastest* that, or *best* whatever: these sorts of characterizations are made all the time, without reflection or irony, and express the confident, self-referential insularity of a society that believes itself to be the measure of those things that matter.

When the outside world enters the American consciousness, it often does so in ways that Americanize and strip the foreignness from experiences, events, and people. Las Vegas is, of course, the extreme case of this phenomenon. Visitors are offered a tour of Europe, ancient Egypt, and exotic locales and cultures from around the world on a strip that features a half-scale replica of the Eiffel Tower and a two-thirds scale Arc de Triomphe, a luminous pyramid and ten-story sphinx, the canals of Venice, an imitation Lake Como, and a castle meant to evoke Arthurian England.

The London Bridge, reassembled as a tourist site in Arizona, the foreign themes and stories that become the backdrop for attractions at Disneyland and Disney World, and the "Hollywoodization" of the foreign and exotic in too many instances to count reflect and reinforce the cultural and spiritual insularity of Americans.

Foreigners, and even some Americans, attribute this insularity to arrogance, to what is thought to be the widely held belief Americans have in the superiority of their culture, way of life, institutions, and accomplishments. This assessment is not, however, quite right. Lyndon Baines Johnson, thirty-sixth president of the United States, is reported to have said that when he visited countries throughout the world, he always had the sense that the foreigners he met envied America and wished in some way to be like, or better yet *be*, Americans. This may sound like jingoism, expressing an insensitive arrogance that critics have said also characterizes George W. Bush and his administration, especially their policy of bringing democracy to Iraq. Such an interpretation is, however, simplistic and inaccurate.

Johnson's naïve attribution of America-envy to foreigners represents what might be characterized as the internalized and unconscious sense Americans have that they *are* history. I would argue that George W. Bush's similar statements should also be taken at face value, as naïve and sincere expressions of a belief that what America has and is, reasonable people anywhere, given a choice, must want. Tocqueville observed this unconscious belief and remarked upon it almost two centuries ago. One might choose to call it arrogance, although Tocqueville did not. Nor does Baudrillard. Both understand that, notwithstanding moments of self-doubt, particularly on the liberal-left, Americans simply assume that their story is the one that truly matters in the world. Their insularity is not borne of arrogance so much as from a naïve faith in the centrality of their experience to human history. Even before America became the world's foremost economic and military power, and long before it became the cultural powerhouse of the world, Americans had incorporated this sense of destiny into their national psyche. This is the thread that connects John Winthrop's "shining city on a hill" to the doctrine of Manifest Destiny and to the statements of every recent president expressing the belief that America has been chosen by God and history to shine a light upon the world.[1] Those who would dismiss such rhetoric as merely political and vulgarly offensive miss the point.

This sense of destiny was expressed by Secretary of State Colin Powell in a 2004 interview. His words resonate with the conviction that America has a mission—even a providential mission—to defend and help spread freedom and democracy in the world, and to oppress evil.

> I think our historical position is that we are a superpower that cannot be touched in this generation by anyone in terms of military power, economic power, the strength of our political system, and our value system. What we would like to see is a greater understanding of the democratic system, the open-market economic system, the rights of men and women to achieve their destiny as God has directed them to do, if they are willing to work for it. And we really do not wish to go to war with people, but, by God, we will have the strongest military around, and that's not a bad thing to have. It encourages and champions our friends that are weak, and it chills the ambitions of the evil. (O'Rourke 2004, 42)

INDIFFERENCE

Given the ignorance and insularity of most Americans, it should come as no surprise to find that they are also largely indifferent to the world beyond their borders. As a general rule, information that is not chiefly about America does not sell and is largely ignored by the news industries that the vast majority of Americans turn to for what is happening beyond their local community. Most American politicians avoid international issues most of the time, knowing that the public is generally indifferent to such matters except when they are packaged in ways that tie them very clearly to local and domestic concerns. Likewise, television news producers and newspaper

---

1. John Winthrop was the first governor of the Massachusetts Bay colony and believed deeply and devoutly that God had divine purpose for that colony. The Doctrine of Manifest Destiny emerged during the 1840s as a justification for the territorial expansion of the United States. The doctrine involved the belief that Providence had destined the United States to expand across North America, spreading democratic ideals and institutions. The poet Walt Whitman captured the spirit of this doctrine when he wrote, "What has miserable, inefficient Mexico—with her superstitions, her burlesque upon freedom, her actual tyranny by the few over the many—what has she to do with the great mission of peopling the new world with a noble race? Be it ours, to achieve that mission!"

editors know that international stories seldom represent the best choice when the goal is to maximize audience size and sell advertising time or space.

Discussing the general and widespread indifference of Americans toward news about the world outside their borders is a classic example of the chicken and the egg dilemma. Which came first, public indifference or the media's apparent aversion to news that is not obviously about the domestic concerns of their American audiences? It is possible that public indifference is caused or at least reinforced by the media's unwillingness to devote much time or resources to international news coverage. But whether the news and public affairs media in the United States are the cause of this indifference or are simply responding to what their customers want to see, hear, and read, it is undeniable that the product they deliver (with some important exceptions) is both largely indifferent toward the world and devotes less coverage to the international scene than the media in many other affluent democracies.

Surveys show that television is the medium Americans rely upon most heavily for their information about national and international current affairs. And although the more literate classes always find this rather shocking, television is also the medium that the majority of people deem most credible and believable. It seems that most people believe the adage "pictures do not lie." Of course they can and often do, and the lies perpetrated by pictures may often have a greater and more enduring impact than those committed by words alone. Some research suggests that the greater credibility people attribute to visual images is biologically rooted (Moyer 1994).

Whatever the explanation, the primary role of television in communicating the information, ideas, and images that most people in the United States and elsewhere rely on for the "pictures in their heads" would seem to be beyond dispute. The 2002 National Geographic survey found that television far outstripped other media as a source for information about world current events among younger American adults (18 to 34 years). Moreover, while television was far and away the most important source of information about world affairs in all of the 10 countries surveyed, Americans were less likely than those in other countries to report relying on other media too for such information. Michael Moore's term "TV Nation"—the title of a cable television program that he created in the 1990s—seems particularly apt in its application to the United States.

Therefore, when discussing the general indifference of most Americans to the world outside their borders, it makes sense to focus on television and how it covers the international scene. This has changed dramatically over the last generation, and most sharply since the early 1990s. These changes may be broken down as follows:

- Less time is devoted to international news stories than in the past, excluding those periods when coverage spikes because of some crisis abroad (for example, the 1990 Gulf War, the 2001 invasion of Afghanistan, and 2003 invasion of Iraq and the subsequent occupation of that country).
- The resources devoted to international reporting have declined dramatically.
- If the Middle East and regions of the world associated with violent hostility toward the United States are excluded from the picture, the rest of the world is, most of the time, virtually invisible when it comes to most American television news coverage. In other words, the world outside the United States is generally portrayed, when it is portrayed at all, as a dangerous place where nasty things happen. (In some ways, of course, this is not especially different from local television news in a city like Detroit or Houston, where the world within a 10-mile radius of most viewers' homes is commonly portrayed as a nasty place where bad things happen.)

The increasing indifference of American television to the outside world is especially reflected in the comparatively paltry resources assigned to its coverage. In 2003, the three traditional networks, ABC, CBS, and NBC, whose evening news programs were watched by about 30 million viewers, all had news bureaus in London, Israel, and Iraq. Only one, ABC, had an office in Africa, and it was staffed by a freelancer. Only one, CBS, had an office in Japan. None had offices in France, Germany, Spain, or anywhere in Asia. Foreign bureaus open and close over the years, of course, in response to the vicissitudes of world events, particularly as these affect American interests. But the trend since the 1980s has been for the world to be reported by and interpreted for American audiences by a television news-gathering system that relies on fewer people on site, deploying diminishing resources. Many of the remaining foreign bureaus of the television networks are staffed chiefly by contract personnel or freelancers. Even when a foreign story *is* covered by one of the regular reporters for a major American network, he

TABLE 1.1	Media Use by Young Adults: News Sources for Current Events, by Country							
	US %	Canada %	France %	Germany %	Italy %	Japan %	Mexico %	Sweden %	UK %
TV News	82	85	89	88	83	93	82	85	84
Newspapers	38	57	47	60	43	49	35	66	64
Radio	13	44	42	58	20	9	29	41	3/
Internet	11	29	18	31	14	20	25	40	20
Magazines	10	23	25	29	15	14	13	41	23

Source: National Geographic-Roper 2002 Global Geographic Literacy Survey (November), 44.

or she may not actually be present at the location that viewers see on their screens. Almost all foreign news bureaus cover a territory that is much broader than the country in which they are located. Thus, all of Asia may be covered from a bureau in Hong Kong, or all of Europe from a bureau in London (Fleeson 2004).

It is common to attribute the shrinkage in the foreign news-gathering capacity of American television networks to economics. The market for international news has become more fragmented and competitive as a result of the ascendance of cable television news and online sources of information. Moreover, the audience for international news tends to be an older demographic that many advertisers do not care to reach. There is, in other words, less money to be made in international news coverage, and therefore the costs devoted to foreign news-gathering have had to be cut.

Declining viewer demand is the key to this explanation. When interest spikes as a result of extraordinary circumstances like the invasion of Afghanistan or the war in Iraq, this temporary boost does not seem to translate into a more enduring general demand for news about the world outside American borders.

Since it burst upon the scene as the broadcaster of record for real-time coverage during the 1990 Gulf War, CNN has had the reputation and enjoyed status of being the television broadcaster that Americans rely on for their pictures and interpretations of the world. But even CNN devotes relatively little in the way of resources to coverage of global affairs, at least compared to such television broadcasters as Britain's BBC or France's state-owned broadcaster, TF1. The model for international coverage used by both the broadcast and cable networks is described by the Organization of American Journalists this way:

> As viewers have left, the network news divisions have shrunk in size. And the priorities about where money goes have shifted. In the process, so has the culture of network news-gathering. What once could be described as organizations with large battalions of experienced correspondents, producers, editors, and camera crews stationed in bureaus worldwide might better be characterized today as organizations with a small pool of high-priced anchors supported by less experienced, less well known correspondents and off-air staffers who can parachute in from afar or assemble satellite footage in New York and cover anything. (The State of the News Media 2004)

INSENSITIVITY

The general indifference of Americans to the world beyond their doorstep masks the fact that, when it comes to interest in and awareness of the international scene, there are really two Americas. There is the America for whom international news is a tough sell, perhaps 80 to 90 per cent of the population, but also an America that follows international news avidly. The Pew Research Center's survey of news consumption refers to this second group as "the core international news audience" and placed its size in 2002 at about 16 per cent of the public, up from about 10 per cent in their 2000 survey (Pew 2002b, 20–21). The members of this group are disproportionately white, male, highly educated, and affluent. Conservative Republicans are as likely as liberal Democrats to say that they follow international affairs "very closely."

Examining the relatively small core audience for international news, one finds that they rely on a much wider range of media than indifferent Americans do for their impressions and information about the world. As figure 1.5 shows, these internationally engaged Americans constitute a disproportionate share of the market for more intensive coverage of public affairs, foreign and domestic.

At the same time, it should be kept in mind that the overall reach of many of these sources of information about the world is quite limited. According

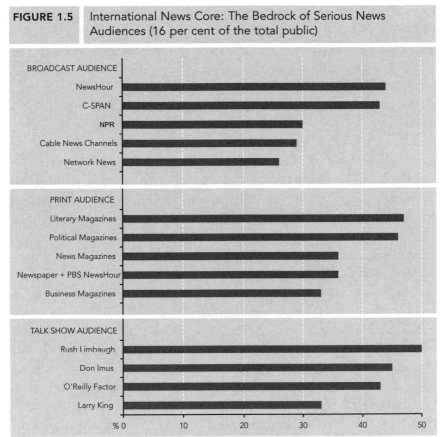

FIGURE 1.5   International News Core: The Bedrock of Serious News Audiences (16 per cent of the total public)

Source: The Pew Center for the People and the Press, Biennial News Consumption Survey (June 9, 2002), 22.

to the Pew Center's 2002 Biennial News Consumption Survey, only about 5 per cent of the American public regularly watch C-Span or PBS's *News Hour*, about 13 per cent regularly read news magazines such as *Time*, *Newsweek*, or *US News & World Report*, and only 2 per cent regularly read serious public affairs and literary magazines like *The Atlantic*, *Harper's* or *The New Yorker* (Pew 2002b). The Sunday morning talk shows, long an anchor for serious discussion of domestic and world affairs on television, draw audiences in the 2 to 4 million range (State of the News Media 2004).

High-quality news sources that do in-depth coverage of issues are supported by a relatively small segment of the American population. Indeed, studies suggest that the same roughly 10 per cent of the population forms the core audience for National Public Radio (NPR), *The New York Times*,

PBS's *News Hour*, the Sunday morning talk shows, C-Span, high-end magazines like *The Atlantic*, and online sources for information on world current affairs. Those Americans who say that they follow international affairs regularly or occasionally are more likely to rely on cable and network news, including both the evening network news programs and morning news shows. As of 2003, the network news programs still had an average combined daily audience of close to 30 million and the morning shows a daily average of 15 million. Cable news programs do much less well, attracting an average of about 2 million viewers during prime time. However, this number obscures the importance of cable television as a news sources for Americans. When asked where they get most of their news about national and international issues, far more people say cable than network television; in 2003 the ratio was about three to one (Pew 2002b). They are, of course, tuning into news programming when it is convenient for them. By repeating the news on a half-hourly basis, providing banners for headlines, and breaking away for live coverage of "action," cable television's 24-hour news cycle enables viewers to watch news when they want it.

When Americans dip in to the information well that the network news programs and cable television news provides, what do they hope to find? The answer is action. Only the relatively small core audience for international news expresses a strong interest in seeing interviews with world leaders, background reports for stories, and, to a certain extent, live news reports. While there is also some interest in live news reports among the vast majority of Americans who follow international news only occasionally or express disinterest, these citizens have very little interest in the sort of reporting that provides context for these live reports.

Whether other national populations are more interested and better informed than Americans when it comes to world affairs is difficult to say with much certainty. The National Geographic survey suggests that while some national populations are, others, including Canadians and Britons, appear to be only marginally more knowledgeable than Americans about the international scene. Knowledge and interest go hand in hand. And, indeed, surveys of the American public demonstrate quite emphatically that, apart from a small segment of the population, most Americans are not very interested in world affairs, and the share of the public that is entirely indifferent—except when terrorists pilot planes into American buildings—is much greater than that which follows international events on a regular basis.

TABLE 1.2 Types of Stories Preferred by Segments of the News Audience

Very interested in...	All %	Core %	Occasional %	Disinterested %
Live news reports	41	71	44	21
Background reports	31	67	32	13
Interviews with world leaders	26	60	25	11
Human interest stories	20	37	20	11
Expert opinions	16	37	15	6

Source: National Geographic-Roper 2002 Global Geographic Literacy Survey (November), 44.

Indifference toward and ignorance of world affairs among Canadians, Britons, or even Russians might be lamentable. But the indifference and ignorance of Americans is altogether different when it comes to the matter of consequences. As the world's most influential country, whose military, corporations, investments, and culture reach all corners of the globe, the prosperity and security of the United States are vitally affected by what happens abroad. But, of course, it is precisely the immense influence of America, combined with an insularity whose roots lie in its history and unconscious faith in its own exceptionalism, that renders Americans largely detached from the world they dominate. This attitude is often characterized as American arrogance, although the prideful disdain this term implies is probably true of only a minority of the population. Insensitivity is a more accurate description for the uninterested incomprehension that a majority of the American public have when it comes to the outside world.

This incomprehension may be seen in the utter failure of Americans to appreciate the gap that exists between their national self-image and the perceptions that other national populations have of them. The enormity of this gap is suggested in figure 1.6. I say "suggested" because this data is derived from a large 11-country survey carried out for the BBC during the winter of 2003, at which point global media coverage of the impending American-led invasion of Saddam Hussein's Iraq was both extensive and overwhelmingly negative. Considerable volatility exists in public opinion toward the United States, and thus one should be wary of generalizations that are based on the sort of snapshot that a one-time survey provides. With this caveat in mind, the findings of the 2003 BBC survey still demonstrate that Americans see themselves and their place in the world very differently from other national populations.

FIGURE 1.6 The Perception Gap: Foreign Perceptions of America and American Perceptions of How Others View Them

A. Thinking about the American military presence in this part of the world, do you agree or disagree that it has helped to bring peace and stability to the area? (Percentage who agree.) (Americans were asked if they agreed that their country's military presence around the world contributed to international peace and stability.)

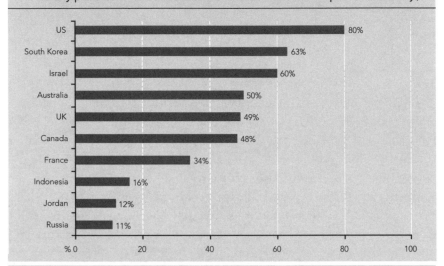

B. Do you think that the way America runs its economy should be copied or not? (Percentage who agree.) (Americans were asked if they thought that other countries wanted to copy the way America runs its economy.)

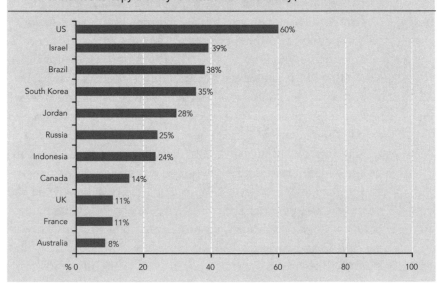

C. If you had the chance, would you like to live in America? (Percentage who respond-
    ed yes.) (Americans were asked if they thought that others wanted to come live in
    America.)

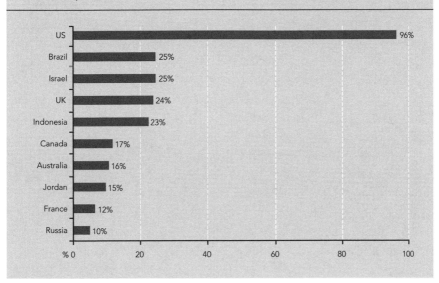

Source: BBC-ICM, "What the World Thinks of America," (June 2003).

CHAPTER TWO

The AMERICAN DREAM MACHINE

"It is safe to say," John Steinbeck wrote, "that the picture of America and Americans which is branded on the minds of foreigners is derived in very large part from our novels, our short stories, *and particularly from our moving pictures*" (Steinbeck 1966, 390; emphasis added). Steinbeck made this observation in 1966, when it was still reasonable to speak of the impact of print and visual media in the same sentence. Even so, Steinbeck the novelist, who also spent many years working for the Hollywood studios of America's dream machine, recognized that the visual images of America exported around the world through film had already supplanted the written word as the chief influence on foreign perceptions of the United States and Americans. What was true then is, of course, even truer today. Foreign opinion leaders and the more educated strata of foreign populations continue to be influenced by the printed word. But in the case of mass opinion abroad, the direct influence of print has been almost entirely eclipsed by visual media. What do they see?

The answer to this question is mixed. It is not the same in all countries, or between different segments of the market within countries. For example, American-made films penetrate more deeply in the German cinema and video rental markets than they do in those of Turkey or Japan. And although American products are overwhelmingly the first choice of both Canadian and British moviegoers, British television viewers are far more likely than Canadians to watch their own domestically produced television shows. In such countries as Argentina, France, and Brazil, American television has only a rather marginal presence, judging by market share, although Hollywood dominates the movie box office in all three of these markets. Sweden has been described by historian Haikan Arvidsson as the most

Americanized country in the world, based on the Swedes' strong taste for American films and television programs.

The American dream machine, it is clear, receives a varied reception in different foreign markets. This variation is particularly great in the case of American-produced television. But in the film industry, Hollywood's international domination is awesome in its scope. Even in societies with cultures, traditions, and lifestyles quite different from those of the United States, including such countries as Japan, Egypt, and Russia, Hollywood either dominates the domestic film market or at least occupies an enormous place within it. For example, box office receipts from Japan for the second weekend of 2004 showed seven American films among the top ten. Four of the top-seven grossing films in Egypt during the first three months of 2004 were Hollywood offerings. When Mel Gibson's *The Passion of the Christ* opened in the Arab world, it steamrolled the competition—as it did in the West, too—running up box office numbers several times greater than its nearest competitor. In most cases, the nearest competitor was also an American-made film (*The Atlantic* 2004, 62).

Table 2.1 shows the number of American films among the top-grossing movies of all time for selected countries. It is clear that when the world seeks to be entertained in front of the big screen—and market studies show that consumer choices in the video rental market mirror those at the cinema—the stories and representations spun by Hollywood's dream machine tend to be the overwhelming favorites.

Surveys conducted by the Pew Center for the People and the Press corroborate the pattern revealed when consumers worldwide vote with their pocketbooks. The Pew's Global Attitudes Survey (2002a) asked representative samples of national populations throughout the world what they liked about America. Most foreign populations readily confessed that they like what Hollywood offers.

Although American television is also well liked abroad, national markets vary considerably in their degree of state control, competition, and openness to foreign programming, through domestic broadcasters and satellite reception. In general, however, these markets have become more open over the last couple of decades due to a combination of deregulation and the development and proliferation of satellite technology that has increased the costs, both economic and political, of trying to limit the choices available to viewers. Homegrown television programs do better, generally speak-

TABLE 2.1	Number of American Films among All-time Top 20 (box-office gross) by Country, February 2004		
Australia	20	Thailand	11/15 **
France	14	UK	17.5 *
Germany	17	World, excluding US	20
Spain	18		

* *Love, Actually*, the twelfth top-grossing film of all time in the UK, was produced jointly by the UK and US.
** Data on the top-15 films only was available for Thailand.
Sources: <http://www.boxofficemojo.com> and <http://www.moviemarshal.com>.

ing, against American competition than is true in the film segment of the entertainment market. Economics appears to be the key factor explaining this difference. The cost of producing, marketing, and distributing an hour of television programming is generally much lower than for cinema. Consequently, the likelihood of domestic producers being able to recoup their costs is greater with television.

Nevertheless, American television is extremely popular in foreign markets throughout the world. Audience share data supplied by agencies such as Neilsen Media Research provides the most reliable measure of the level of American penetration into foreign television markets. In some countries, however, such information can be difficult or even impossible to acquire. Where it does exist, these ratings data show that American television programs are very popular. At the extreme end, if sports and news programs are excluded, about 90 per cent of prime-time television viewing in English-speaking Canada is devoted to American programs. But even in countries where the language barrier is higher, including Germany, Sweden, the Netherlands, and France, American shows capture a large share of the television market. Indeed, it is common for some channels in foreign markets to be devoted principally to the broadcast of American programs, at least during prime viewing hours, with sub-titles or dubbing in the language of the foreign viewing-audience. According to Neilsen's ratings, on a typical evening of television in Sweden (April 16, 2004), privately owned TV3 showed almost nothing but American sitcoms, dramas, and movies between 7 p.m. and midnight, including *The Simpsons*, *8 Simple Rules*, *Jim's World*, and *Two and a Half Men*. Sweden's TV4, another of the country's most-watched channels, included *Malcolm in the Middle*, *Band of Brothers*, and *NYPD Blue* in its evening schedule for that same day. Kanal 5 broadcast nothing but American programs that evening, followed in the wee hours by a rerun of *The Tonight Show with Jay Leno*. Even state-owned SVT1 included American programming, the film *Space Cowboys*, during its prime-time line-up.

On that same day, according to Neilsen, Germany offered viewers a choice of nine different American films during prime time on cable channels. These included *Patriot Games, Sphere, Christine, Maximum Risk, American Psycho II*, and others. Even in France, the amount of American programming on cable television was prodigious. It included such films as *Goldmember* and *Independence Day*, and the television programs *Friends, Stargate, Buffy the Vampire Slayer, Jackass*, and *The Jerry Springer Show*. In Russia, where the number of cable television channels is still comparatively limited, American programs also do well. During a typical week in March 2003, six of the top-twenty program ratings went to American shows. These included *Who Wants to Be a Millionaire* (twice), *Jackass* (three times), and the film *The Matrix*.

Further illustration would only be tedious. While the degree of American penetration in foreign television markets varies considerably across affluent Western societies, it is significant in all of them. The cultural barrier is higher in some regions of the world, and the indigenous television industries of some countries are better able than others to compete with relatively inexpensive and culturally seductive American programs. But even in markets whose languages and values might be thought hostile or at least unreceptive to American television, the stories, characters, and perhaps above all, the style communicated through the small screen often attract a sizeable audience (see Box 2.1).

The soundtrack to life throughout the world is also heavily Americanized, although its degree of saturation and its consequences are almost certainly less pronounced than with film and television. American recording artists are routinely among the most popular in countries throughout the world. Figure 2.1 shows the number of American recording artists or groups that placed among the top 10 singles in selected countries at the beginning of April 2004. Hip-hop, rap, and the star-brand genre of pop rock represented by such singers as Britney Spears and Madonna were among the most popular American music exports.

Not only in Western countries is American music is an important part of daily life. Driving along the streets of Amman, Jordan on a Friday

BOX 2.1   American Television Programs in Egypt

Egypt has eight local channels, collectively entitled Television al Masri (Egyptian TV), all of which are state controlled. Each day they open and close with Quranic recitations. Many have Islamic broadcasts in the morning hours. These channels vary in the amount of American programming they show from quite a lot to none.

In addition to local television programming, Egypt also owns a series of channels for satellite distribution, called Nile Satellite. Nile has 16 different stations. Arabic Radio and Television (ART) stations comprise the majority of them. There is ART Tarab, which plays Arabic music and classic Arabic singers all day. ART Muzika shows Arabic music videos. ART Hakayat (stories) broadcasts various Arabic soap operas all day. Egyptian soap operas are different in nature than American ones. They do not revolve solely around romances, but involve tales of family life, problems, and friendships. They are more like *Seventh Heaven* in the US than soaps, such as *Days of Our Lives*. ART Aflam (movies) shows Arabic movies all day.

However, Nile Satellite also offers Film Channel, which shows only American movies (but not recent releases). Nile Satellite's Movies Channel shows a mix of old and new, obscure and more popular American movies and programs. Movie Channel 2 has a similar format. Super Movies channel features Western films. Nile Munowat (Mix) broad-

casts Western music videos. TV Land has shows like *The Late Show with David Letterman*, *Survivor*, *NYPD Blue*, *Alias*, and *Ripley's Believe It or Not*. Nile Satellite also devotes a couple of ART channels to sports. In addition to soccer and other local sports, they show American wrestling and American and British soccer leagues, as well as the American Women's Soccer League.

Nile Satellite also has a channel for family and children's programs. However, none of them seem to have originated in America. Nile Iktiqafa (education) also has nothing American. In addition to Nile, there are other satellite channels in Egypt, including Orbit and Arab Satellite. Arab Satellite broadcasts a variety of channels, such as CNN, BBC Prime, and MBC and LBC (Lebanese channels), as well as the Disney Channel and Egypt Satellite 1 and 2. Moreover, it has American Blast and Star Movies, which both feature American programming. American Blast broadcasts shows such as *Smallville*, *The Sopranos*, *The Bachelor*, *The Bachelorette*, *Gilmore Girls*, *Murder She Wrote*, and others. MTV and Paramount are also available.

Finally, many Egyptian programs are based on (or are imitations of) various American shows such as *Candid Camera*, *America's Funniest Videos*, and even *Baywatch*.

Source: Based on information from Egypt TV, <http://www.mytravelguide.com/city-guide/Africa-&-Middle-East/Egypt/Egyptian-TV>; Masrawy TV Guide, <http://tv.masrawy.com> (accessed May 19, 2004); and BBC News, "Baywatch Gets Egyptian Treatment," <http://news.bbc.co.uk/1/hi/entertainment/tv_and_radio/3039751.stm>. Information compiled and translated by Crystal Ennis.

evening, the sound of hip-hop and rap will certainly be heard coming from the cars of young males. Mohamed Al-Jazeera, disk jockey at Radio Jordan in Amman, puts it this way: "When it comes to [my young listeners], it's either the beat, or the reality of the song, or they're infatuated by how Tupac used to look, or Eminem" (BBC, 2003).

Younger people in particular are more likely than those who entered adulthood before the computer revolution to devote a significant share of

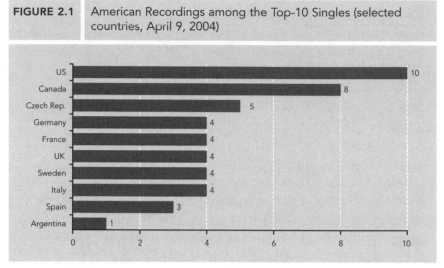

FIGURE 2.1 American Recordings among the Top-10 Singles (selected countries, April 9, 2004)

Source: VNU eMedia & Information Marketing, <http://www.billboard.com>.

their media-consuming time to the Internet and to computer and video games. It is widely believed that the Internet and the explosive growth in the video game industry have extended the cultural dominance of America abroad. Ziauddin Sardar's argument that the creation and colonization of cyberspace is overwhelmingly an American enterprise is representative of this view:

> Cyberspace did not appear ... from nowhere.... It is the conscious reflection of the deepest desires, aspirations, experiential yearning, and spiritual angst of Western man; it is resolutely designed as a new market and is an emphatic product of the culture, world view, and technology of Western civilization.... Cyberspace, then, is the "American dream" writ large; it marks the dawn of a new "American civilization." ... Cyberspace is particularly geared up towards the erasure of all non-Western histories. (Sardar, quoted in Dodge and Kitchin 2000, 41)

It may be more accurate, however, to argue that these relatively new media have done nothing to reduce the cultural influence of America. An examination of Internet traffic shows that, on the whole, Web sites tend to be dominated by domestic users. Swedes surf Swedish sites, Brits surf British sites, and the French have an overwhelming preference for French sites.

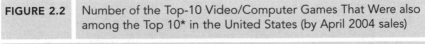

FIGURE 2.2 Number of the Top-10 Video/Computer Games That Were also among the Top 10* in the United States (by April 2004 sales)

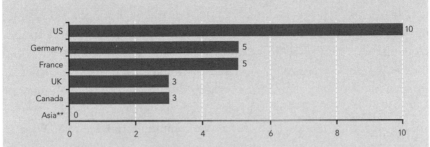

* As of mid-April 2004, this top 10 included Battlefield Vietnam, Far Cry, MVP Baseball 2004, Nascar Racing 2003, NBA Ballers, Harvest Moon: A Wonderful Life, Pokemon Colosseum, Syberia 2, Tom Chancy's Splinter Cell, and Unreal Tournament 2004.

** The Asian market, as reported at YesAsia.com, includes China, Japan, Singapore, and Hong Kong. There was no overlap between the most popular games in this large market and the American market. The Sims, popular in Western Europe, was also a top-selling computer game in Asia.

Sources: Amazon.com; Amazon.ca; Amazon.co.uk; Amazon.dc; Amazon.fr; YesAsia.com (accessed April 20, 2004).

Language also plays a very strong role in determining the Internet preferences of a national population, reinforced by the fact that much of what Internet users are searching for (excluding porn, one of the most popular uses) is information about local sports, news, and shopping. In their analysis of the geography of cyberspace, Martin Dodge and Rob Kitchin conclude that the globalizing and homogenizing dynamics of Internet usage coexist alongside dynamics rooted in more traditional identities of place and community (Dodge and Kitchin 2000, 34–36). The claim that the technology of PC-based communications is culturally homogenizing, and even Americanizing, is not entirely true.

Those in their twenties today represent the first generation to have grown up spending much of their time playing computer and video games. While it appears that there is a powerful American presence in this market, there are also clear and persistent indications of cross-national differences in preferences. Figure 2.2 shows the numbers on the top-selling video and computer games in selected Western countries, as recorded through Amazon's online sales in each of these markets.

Several of the top-selling games in these foreign markets that were not among the best-selling games in the United States when the survey was taken were also American. These included Grand Theft Auto, Gran Turismo 4, and Final Fantasy. But there were also indications of national differences in game preferences. The most striking was the considerable popularity of The Sims in France, Germany, and the UK. Described on Amazon UK as a "people management game ... [that] allows you to create, direct, and manage the lives of Sim City's residents ..." the Sims games have not made a serious dent in the American market. It is tempting to conclude that Americans' coolness toward games that stress cooperation and interacting with others (e.g., basic needs of Sim City residents are met by interacting with other Sims) in ways that do not involve simply killing or otherwise defeating them is evidence of the greater individualism of American culture compared to the more communitarian spirit of Western European gamers. However, based on such meager evidence, this would be a rather far-reaching generalization.

OPINION LEADERS AND THEIR AUDIENCES

Like their fellow citizens, those who belong to the more educated and politically interested and active strata of a national population watch television, go to the cinema, rent videos, and listen to music. Even more than their fellow citizens, they are likely to have at least one PC at home and to use one on a regular basis at work. It is one of the characteristic features of mass consumer societies—sometimes referred to as affluent middle-class societies—that the tastes of different social classes exhibit broad similarities. The appeal of Friends, the music of Jennifer Lopez, and the movies of Russell Crowe or Julia Roberts cuts across class lines. This phenomenon is found in the United States and other countries as well. At the same time, however, there are some significant differences in the media consumption habits of different strata of the population. The more educated, affluent, and civically engaged are more likely than less educated, less affluent, and less politically interested and active segments of the population to rely on newspapers and public-affairs oriented magazines for information, to read books, and to have learned about the world at university. They inhabit a world of information that is denser than that of their fellow citizens and in which explanation—identifying reasons, determining causality, and attributing motive—occupies an important place. However, in other countries throughout the world, the idea/information milieu created by opinion leaders for their engaged and informed national audiences tends to be significantly different from that in the United States.

This difference can be measured in many ways. Box 2.2 contains the reflections of Love Edquist, a highly educated young Swede asked to identify the main influences on his ideas about the United States and Americans. I have also asked foreign students from countries around the world, including China, India, France, and Belgium to engage in this reflective exercise. Invariably, newspapers and television news are acknowledged to be important sources of information about America. Classes taken at university, taught by non-Americans, are often mentioned as influential sources of perceptions as well. All the foreign nationals whom I have asked to reflect on the sources of their early impressions of America had, to varying degrees, seen American movies and television and listened to American music during their youth. This is something they have in common with the general population of their respective countries. But layered on top of this body of general impressions, images, and ideas about America is the act of *interpretation*. Interpretation is the process of making sense of information, giving it structure, formulating explanations, and determining its more general significance. A Hollywood film such as *Spider-Man* or an episode of *Friends* provides an interpretation of America at some level, both intellectually and emotionally, even when the story is not ostensibly about America. But the special interpretive role of media such as newspapers, books written about the United States by foreigners for foreign markets, and the televised news and public affairs programs broadcast in countries outside America is to *select* and *frame* information in a way that says, "This is important to an understanding of America, and this is why things happen as they do."

Those who have lived abroad and managed to break out of the America-centric media milieu provided by the *International Herald Tribune*, CNN International, and their preferred online American news Web sites will know that the world looks very different when viewed through the eyes of foreign media and the opinion leaders who interpret it. Not only is the world not seen through the prism of American values, preoccupations, and interests, but when it is covering an issue that is also being covered in the United States, the account is often unrecognizable as the same story. This is most obviously and dramatically the case when international crises like the war in Iraq or the ongoing struggle between Israel and the Palestinians are covered. But it is also true when it comes to day-to-day coverage of the

---

BOX 2.2   "My Relationship to America": A Swedish View

Is it possible to have a relationship to a country you have never visited? It seems that more or less all adults on Earth have some kind of relationship to America, even though many of them never set foot in the country. Prior to the year I spent in North America, I was included in this group. I had never been in the US; I had not even been on the other side of the Atlantic, and still I had very distinct opinions about the American society, and American politics.

Growing up, as I did, in Sweden gives people some kind of a dual connection to America, as most of the countries in the world have. Sweden has some kind of love-hate relationship to the US. On the one hand, Sweden, as a social democratic welfare society, sees the US as the most negative example of what a market-oriented capitalist society represents. But at the same time, we admire the US for its economic, political, and technological success.

Swedish people are in general pretty well-informed about the world outside, but they are particularly well-informed about the US. Sweden, as more or less all countries on Earth, is more concerned about the US than about any other country in the world. Visit a Swedish workplace for a week, and you can be sure that the US will be discussed at least once. Visit a Swedish high school, and ask them about their opinion of the US; all of them would probably present a pretty well-

detailed opinion about the American society and American politics. But why do so many people in Sweden have distinct opinions about the US? I think that the answer can be found in the different relationship Sweden has had to the US. As an officially neutral country, Sweden did not join any side of the Cold War. Sweden was also not directly involved in World War II, and by that did not owe the US the same gratefulness as the other European countries did. Sweden has never been directly politically dependent on the US, although the economic importance of the US has always been great to Sweden. Sweden's independence from American politics gave Sweden a more independent relationship to the US than other European nations, and because of that it has been legitimate for politicians to criticize the US in public.

Today, Sweden's relationship to the US can be viewed as skeptical, although probably not as skeptical as the French or the German view is. I think that the Swedish relationship to the US differs in respect to other countries on both sides of the former iron curtain in Europe. I think that Sweden's relationship can be seen as a bit more "mature" than the rest of Europe's because Sweden has been criticizing the US from the days of the Vietnam War. In the rest of Europe, more general criticism against the US has only been possible after the end of the Cold War.

Source: Personal interview with Love Edquist 2004. Used by permission.

---

news. The nature and extent of these differences and their consequences for America's relations with the world are the subjects of chapters 3, 4, and 5.

One way to get a sense of the gap that separates America's more educated and engaged citizens from their counterparts abroad is to examine the books that they read. There is some overlap, but relatively little, especially when compared to the extent to which American cultural products penetrate foreign film, television, and popular music markets. As a general rule, national book-buying publics prefer to read about themselves, or at least to read books written by their compatriots. An examination of best-selling nonfiction titles in 2002 in Argentina, Germany, India, and the United States finds hardly any overlap in the ten most popular books in these four national markets. While Americans were reading Michael Moore's *Stupid White Men*, Woodward's *Bush at War*, and Rudolph Giuliani's *Leadership: How to Run Your Business Like the Greatest City in the World*, Argentines were reading *The Road of Tears* (a self-discovery book written by an Argentine psychotherapist), *The Atrocious Charm of Being Argentine*, and *Juan Manuel de Rosas* (an account of the rule of a nineteenth-century Argentine dictator). Germans were somewhat less nationalist in their tastes, reading Stephen Hawking's *The Universe in a Nutshell* and Spencer Johnson's *Who Moved My Cheese?* But they also bought *The Chancellor Lives in the Swimming Pool*, a book about German politics; *The Manns*, a biography of the German writer and his family; and *The Great Escape*, a book about ethnic Germans who fled their Eastern European homelands toward the end of World War II. At the same time, Indians were reading books mainly about India and mainly by Indian writers, including *The Algebra of Infinite Justice* by Arundhati Roy, *A Hundred Encounters* by Sham Lal, and *Pakistan History and Politics, 1947–71* by M. Rafique Afzal (Christian Science Monitor 2002; All Bookstores 2004).

It occasionally happens that a particular book that is popular in America captures the international imagination—at least in the West—and becomes widely read in many countries. Dan Brown's *The Da Vinci Code* achieved this feat in 2004. Michael Moore's books *Stupid White Men* and *Dude, Where's My Country?* experienced some considerable success in the UK, Germany, and Canada, fuelled by and in turn fuelling the anti-Bush administration sentiment that increased in these countries after about 2002. But on the whole, national book-reading publics prefer to read about themselves and about events and experiences closer to home. If one looks at the best-selling books in a non-Western society like China, there is virtually no trace of American, or, for that matter, Western influence on the reading tastes of the population (see, for example, the lists of bestsellers provided at <www.yesasia.com>).

Not only do the more educated strata of different societies tend to read non-Americans books, but the information, images, and ideas they encounter in newspapers and magazines, and the news that they watch on television and hear on the radio, ranges from significantly to enormously different from what is experienced by their US counterparts. Simply put, the news and public affairs universes inhabited by opinion leaders and those who consume their products vary considerably across societies. American films, television, music, brand advertising, and products all have ideas about America embedded in them. But news and public affairs programming produced abroad is different in two important ways. First, it tends to be produced by non-Americans for a non-American market. Second, it purports to provide an objective representation of America, an interpretation anchored in the reality of facts.

One of the lessons that at least some Americans learned leading up to the 2003 invasion of Iraq and the subsequent period of occupation was that the way in which these events were portrayed outside the United States was dramatically different from the domestic representations of these same events. During the month-long campaign that preceded the fall of Baghdad to American and British troops, American viewers and newspaper readers saw images and read stories of combat and casualties that were quite different from those seen and read in the Arab world. Coverage in Arab countries was dominated by bloody scenes of Iraqi civilian casualties; stories of allegedly indiscriminate and perhaps deliberate American—it was generally represented as American, rather than Anglo-American—bombings of hospitals, schools, homes, and markets; and an interpretation of American motivation that combined the desire to conquer and control Iraq's oil wealth with Israeli-Zionist influence in Washington. This was not, needless to say, the dominant picture that the American media provided at home (see box 2.3).

The role of al-Jazeera, the Qatar-based broadcaster that has acquired the reputation and status of being the CNN of the Arab world, has become much discussed in the United States. It has been accused by critics of inflaming hatred toward the United States through its choice of images from the war in Iraq and its interpretation of American actions and motives.

But while media coverage in the Arab and Muslim worlds became a hot topic of discussion in the United States, most Americans remained blithely ignorant of the tone and nature of war coverage in other parts of the world. It is probably fair to say that the unprecedentedly massive anti-war demonstrations that occurred across Europe in February 2003 would not have been either as large or extensive had it not been for the overwhelmingly negative coverage of American motives in the media of these countries leading up to the war.

BOX 2.3   "A Picture Tells Where the Paper Is Published"

To some measure, the world's geography can be mapped by assessing the photographs on the front pages of newspapers published during the war in Iraq. Is the main picture an image of a surrendering Iraqi soldier? Good chance it is an American daily. A picture of a weeping Iraqi civilian? Likely European. And if the civilian is bleeding horribly, there's a good chance it is one of the Malaysian dailies.

Although several European and a few American papers chose a picture of celebrating Iraqis surrounding a downed US Apache helicopter, it was a particularly popular photograph in the Middle East media yesterday.

If the paper has a photo of a regal-looking Saddam Hussein, the Iraqi leader, along with other shots of disfigured bodies, apparently civilians killed by US bombs, then you are likely looking at *Babil*, a daily owned by Saddam's son Uday....

The difference in style and substance of the world's media was captured by the main headline on yesterday's *Le Figaro* of Paris: "Images of war, warring images."

Source: Adrian Humphreys, *National Post*, 18 March 2003.

The high degree of American influence that one finds in countries throughout the world when it comes to film, television, music, and what might be described as lifestyle, does not exist in the news media. Americanization appears to stop at the doorstep of the system whose role it is to purvey what are generally believed to be fact-based representations and interpretations of America. The same may be said for national education systems, including the universities attended by those who go on to become the opinion leaders and elites of their societies. In some countries, such as Cuba, much of the Middle East, and North Korea, what is taught about the United States is overwhelmingly negative. This is, of course, not surprising in countries and regions where relations with the United States have been hostile over a considerable period of time. It is even less surprising in societies where information is carefully controlled and used for state propaganda. But even in free societies where relations with the United States have been generally friendly over time, critical portrayals and negative representations—of policies, history, culture, and involvement in the world—are quite common and, moreover, systematically integrated into the teaching curriculum. This phenomenon is well demonstrated in Dana Lindaman and Kyle Ward's recent book *History Lessons: How Textbooks from around the World Portray US History* (2004). Box 2.4 explains how the United States is portrayed in the history textbooks used by its northern neighbor, Canada.

BOX 2.4   Teaching about America: The Case of Canada

Textbooks used in Canadian schools throughout the twentieth century portrayed the United States as dishonorable, churlish, and even bullying, a new study says.

America received a reprieve after the Second World War, when course materials portrayed the nation as a champion of democracy taking on the Communist threat, but it was short-lived.

"In the early part of the twentieth century, there's a sense of moral superiority in our treatment, and it's coming from a conservative education elite," Amy von Heyking, a professor of education at the University of Alberta, said in an interview.

"By the end of the century, there's the same sense of cultural and even moral superiority—we as Canadians understand the world—but it's now coming from a left education establishment."

"We are quite self-righteous that we know America in a way they don't know us, but it's a superficial look. We use them for our own purposes," said Ms. Von Heyking, who undertook a content analysis of curriculum documents and 75 textbooks used in Canadian history, geography, civics, and social studies courses in elementary and secondary schools.

Source: Sarah Schmidt, "Textbooks Portrayed Americans as Bullies: Study," *National Post*, 5 June 2004, A4.

It goes without saying that a fair representation of the United States cannot ignore the dark and dirty corners of America's past and present. No American high school government teacher or university professor of political science worthy of the position would teach his or her subject matter as an unadulterated story of spotless virtue, justice, and triumphalism. There is no reason to expect non-American teachers to be less critical. However, the evidence suggests that they are much more critical and that the information, ideas, and images of the United States that they communicate to their students reinforce the generally critical characterizations and interpretations that dominate the news and public affairs programming of their countries.

Those who produce the news around the world make their decisions about what to cover and how to interpret it based on a constellation of factors quite different from that which prevails in the United States. This rather obvious fact is enormously important to understanding how and why America is portrayed the way it is in particular countries and regions of the world. Those who construct the news, including journalists, producers, editors, photographers, camera crews, and researchers, are influenced by their own knowledge, values, and beliefs; by the organizational settings within which they work; and by the expectations of those who ultimately determine whether they will be able to achieve their professional, financial, and other goals. Journalists, editors, and producers operating within the state-controlled media system of North Korea clearly respond to a different set of factors in selecting and framing stories about the United States than do, say, those at the French newspaper *Le Monde* or the state-owned BBC in the United Kingdom. In order to explain the information and images communicated to national audiences about America, one needs to understand the particular configuration of ideas, interests, and institutions that characterize a country's or region's media system. Figure 2.3 shows a simplified model of the factors that ultimately shape public opinion.

The processes and paths that lead to public opinion toward the United States are not as simple as figure 2.3 might suggest. Moreover, their specific characteristics vary considerably across countries. Who the information/ image generators—or more simply, opinion leaders—are in each country, why they produce their information, for what purposes and in response to what motivations, and based on what knowledge will be quite different in Canada compared to China, for example. The existence and degree of competition and variation between segments of the information/image-generating class will also vary between countries.

Likewise, the structure and attributes of the information/image communication system in different countries also vary enormously and differ in their specific impacts on what is communicated, how it is communicated, and to whom. These systems range from the pluralistic and free end to those that are monolithic and tightly controlled, as is characteristic of totalitarian states. The relative importance of the media, schools, the state, and institutions such as religious organizations, social movements, political parties, interest groups, and labor unions in disseminating information and ideas about America and influencing public opinion varies significantly across societies. These linkage mechanisms connecting opinion leaders to the general public are crucially important. They also determine the circulation of information and ideas among current opinion leaders and influence the intellectual and attitudinal formation of future ones. Ultimately, these links determine what points of view, interpretations, and pictures of America reach the idea/information-consuming public.

Finally, the image of America held by the members of a national population—the dependent variable in this model—is often quite complex and segmented. For example, it has long been known that elites in Western European societies have, for centuries, tended to be less positively disposed toward America than their general populations (Ferrero 1913). In some

FIGURE 2.3	Image of America: Basic Interpretive Model for General Populations

ELITES	LINKAGE MECHANISMS	ELITE & MASS OPINION
INFORMATION/IMAGE GENERATORS	STRUCTURE & NATURE OF INFO/IMAGE COMMUNICATION SYSTEM	IMAGE OF AMERICA
Educators	Media System	Perceptions
Opinion Leaders	Political System	Sentiments
Politicians	Education System	Beliefs
INDEPENDENT VARIABLES*	INTERVENING VARIABLES*	DEPENDENT VARIABLE

* The feedback loop between the "Elites" and "Linkage Mechanisms" variable categories is intended to underline the fact that both of these may operate as independent variables. By labeling these linkage mechanisms as intervening variables, I do not mean to suggest that the structures and processes included here may not also have a causal impact on elites, their selection, and value/belief formation.

countries, including Canada and the United Kingdom, the idea/information-generating class is and has long been divided in how it portrays and assesses the United States. In a country like South Korea, there is a considerable divide between generations when it comes to public opinion toward America. And in virtually all countries, it is important to recognize conflicting ideas, beliefs, and sentiments that people have toward different aspects of America. Admiration for what are thought to be particular American traits, values, historical figures and events, or accomplishments can coexist with a lively dislike or even hatred of other traits or motives ascribed to America or its government, particular policies or actions, and specific influences believed to be exerted by American governments, businesses, culture, or other institutions.

The model of how information, beliefs, and attitudes are acquired and communicated presented in figure 2.3 is that of a developed, literate society, to a large degree. It assumes the importance of certain processes of communication and the prominence of certain categories of opinion leaders. More specifically, it strongly suggests that we ought to be paying attention to the publicly expressed views of media, state, and cultural elites. Their views will be expressed in ways likely to influence mass opinion on television, in print journalism, books, and films, and in instructional materials used in schools.

But what about a society like Pakistan, where the literacy rate is about 45 per cent and only 4 per cent of households have a television? Or India, where the literacy rate is a bit higher (about 60 per cent) and over 90 per cent of households do not have television? In such societies, where do average people—many of whom cannot read, have never or seldom watched television, and are only loosely connected to the globalized media system—get their ideas and information about America?

Some will say that it does not matter. To the extent that the attitudes and beliefs of such people have little or no impact on the policies of those who govern them, what they think about America is of no consequence. But it is not necessarily true that the opinions of the masses, even in a repressive society, do not matter. If the ability of a regime to maintain its grip on power and resist domestic threats to its dominance depends partly on the vilification of America—Iran's mullahs come to mind—and the need to occasionally draw on this hostile sentiment to mobilize public support, the opinions of the masses will indeed matter.

But even if a regime is not particularly hostile toward the United States and does not need to mobilize anti-Americanism to counter challenges to its hold on power, the sentiments and ideas of the masses may still matter. This is illustrated in a story that Orhan Pamuk tells of an encounter that he had with an illiterate shopkeeper in Istanbul, just after 9/11. This man, who seldom watched television, saw the scenes of the planes slicing through the World Trade Center and the towers collapsing. He heard that this was the work of Islamic terrorists. With no prompting, according to Pamuk, he said, "They were right to do this." Pamuk calls this the "anger of the damned," borne of a resentment that is generated by poverty and the belief that America is in some way to blame for the condition of despair that people like this shopkeeper and his neighbors experience (Pamuk 2001). Leaving aside for now the matter of the validity of Pamuk's thesis about the roots of anti-Americanism in some societies, another question arises from the shopkeeper's vehement response: How did he develop this particular image of America as an enemy to people like him and the cause of his miserable condition? He did not acquire it at school, or from reading newspapers or Internet sites, or from watching television or Hollywood films. Whose images and interpretations, and what information communicated through what means, shaped his ideas about and sentiments toward America? Who are the opinion leaders in his world?

Traditional forms of communication, person-to-person and channeled through community leaders such as imams and other spiritual guides, rather than the modern mass media are the key to explaining the attitudes and beliefs of people like this shopkeeper and the large majority in societies like Pakistan and India who live in households without television or the Internet. But this does not mean that modern forms of communication are not significant in such societies. Even in societies like these, there are Internet cafés and educated classes who participate in the global communication system. The result is a combination of high-tech and low-tech opinion formation/dissemination systems that, while not totally separate from one another, add up to a very different model than that which exists in more affluent, highly literate societies.

The consequences that follow from this are important and may be illustrated with two examples. First, in 2002 the US State Department organized and financed a television advertising campaign called Shared Values, targeted at Muslim populations in the Middle East. The ads were met with a wall of skepticism and mistrust. What came to be seen as the failure of the Shared Values campaign was blamed mainly on the way the ads were constructed. Without minimizing the importance of the cognitive obstacles that must be overcome when delivering a message that is sharply at odds with the prevailing image held by the targeted audience, the whole idea of a television-based campaign to capture the hearts and minds of hostile populations may be based on a flawed premise. This premise is that when it comes to opinion formation, television has the same importance in the targeted societies as it does in wealthy societies where television is a leading medium for communicating information and images about the world. This may be a reasonable premise regarding Kuwait, but a seriously inaccurate one for Indonesia.

Pakistan provides a second example that shows the danger of generalizing a rich-country/literate-population model of idea formation and dissemination to a very different society. After the overthrow of the Taliban in Afghanistan, followed by the lead-up to and invasion of Iraq, a movement to boycott companies and products associated with the United States gained momentum in Pakistan. It was spearheaded by the Islamist Party, supported by imams throughout the country, and encouraged by Muslim entrepreneurs who wished to challenge the dominance of Coca-Cola with alternative "Muslim colas." It is difficult to know how much damage the boycott did, but it is probably significant that the head of Coca-Cola's Eurasia and Middle East division, Ahmet Bozer, acknowledged that his company's sales had been affected and that it was engaged in a public relations campaign to counter negative associations that the boycott might create in the minds of consumers. Coca-Cola's public relations campaign was largely urban-based and relied on billboards and electronic ads, including television and radio. Although the evidence is rather fragmentary, the anti-American boycott appeared to be more effective outside of major urban centers and to have had the least support from middle-class, educated Pakistanis. There are, of course, many possible explanations for the varying levels of success the campaign achieved with different groups. But it is certainly possible that Coca-Cola's efforts to blunt the effects of the boycott were more effective in parts of the market and with segments of the population that rely on modern means for idea formation and dissemination.

In the final analysis, the point is very simple. Any attempt to change or even reinforce an idea or image about America needs to be tailored to the way people in the targeted society acquire these ideas and images. In a society where the opinions of local notables, spiritual leaders, or teachers are more important than television or newspapers in shaping what people think, efforts to change people's beliefs and sentiments ought to appeal to these opinion leaders. Television ads will probably be beside the point.

* * *

In an age when American isolation from the rest of the world is simply not an option and global scrutiny of America and of those who are seen to embody its values, institutions, and policies is increasingly intense and unremitting—and probably less forgiving— impressions of America and Americans matter more than ever before. Events since the terrorist attacks of September 11, 2001, have demonstrated that public opinion outside of America has a direct and sometimes decisive impact on the ability of the United States to pursue its foreign policy objectives and on the reputation and credibility of America throughout the world. The term *weaponization of information*, used by US military officials and others during the occupation of Iraq, captured the increasingly crucial importance of information, ideas, and images in the battle for public opinion. Although the deployment of information has long been essential to the achievement of a country's foreign policy objectives, particularly during periods of war, it has arguably become more important than ever. The televised pictures of abused Iraqi prisoners in May 2004 generated a firestorm of criticism literally across the world, demonstrating the power of images to seize the public's attention and influence public opinion. What Neil Postman calls "the seductions of the image," alerts us to both the significance of visual media in shaping ideas and behaviors and, moreover, the special challenges posed by visual representations of reality (Postman, cited in Moyer 1994).

To understand this point, imagine for a minute that instead of relying on televised images of Iraqi prisoners in degrading sexual positions and naked on a leash held by a female American soldier, the claims and evidence of abuse were based entirely on print and oral testimony. Imagine further that this evidence came from an organization like the Red Cross, from American soldiers, and from Iraqis claiming to have witnessed or experienced it. As important and reinforcing as such testimony and evidence might prove, can there be any doubt that the images depicting these actions resonated far more powerfully and widely than mere words ever could have done? The reality that matters, or that matters most, is that which people can see in what Stuart Ewan calls their "eye's mind." Postman goes so far as to say that when the word squares off with the image, the image wins hands-down:

> The environment created by language and the printed word has been moved to the periphery of the culture—especially print—and at its center the image has taken over, mostly the television image but not only the TV image. This is a culture that is inundated by visual images—advertising, the works. (Postman, cited in Moyer 1994)

Postman is talking here about America and other affluent societies whose prosperity is based on mass consumption. But the point he makes about the generally superior power of the image in a contest with the word seems to apply wherever the members of a population have come to rely on visual media, especially television, for their information about and understanding of the world. Images—the stories they tell and the meanings they ascribe to events—have become what Postman characterizes as a new form of discourse that is seductive precisely because its ability to influence and persuade does not depend solely, or even primarily, on logic, rationality, or the

PLATE 2.1 The power of pictures. This famous photo and several like it, taken at Abu Ghraib prison in Iraq, conveyed an unflattering image of America throughout the world.

standards of truth and falsity that would generally be used to assess a written or oral claim. Here is a picture of a naked Iraqi soldier on the end of a leash being held by a young female American solider. The explanation of how matters reached this point and what the context—institutional, sexual, cultural, psychological—is for this image matter far less in terms of their impact on public opinion than the image itself. John Gabrieli, a Stanford psychologist, suggests that the supremacy of images over words may well be biologically rooted. He notes that the human species evolved in response to images and that the written word and even oral explanations of our environment are relatively recent in evolutionary terms (Moyer 1994).

But as important as images have become in shaping and supplying what Walter Lippman long ago called "the pictures in our heads" (1922), they have not rendered irrelevant or insignificant other ways of representing the world. Opinion leaders—including those who select the images that are communicated through visual media and decide how they are organized and for what purposes, and whose preferences and choices influence the representation of reality that is conveyed by the pictures—tend to be anchored in a cognitive world in which print and oral modes of knowing and communicating "truth" continue to be important.

CHAPTER THREE

MASS *and* ELITE PERCEPTIONS *of* AMERICA

Long before the "idea of America" broke upon the general consciousness of the world, originally as a place to immigrate and eventually as a power whose military, movies, music, and money spanned the globe, elites were aware of what they called the New World. *Mundis novis* and *de orbe novo* were the terms used by educated literate classes of Western Europe to describe the Americas after Columbus's voyages of discovery. The idea of America gripped the imaginations of ruler and thinkers. Rulers envisioned it as a place rich in resources and territory that could add to the strength and grandeur of their empires; thinkers viewed it as a dramatic challenge to established ways of knowing about the human condition. As J. Martin Evans argues in *America: The View from Europe*, the discovery of the Americas challenged the notion of limitation, which was simply assumed to be a characteristic of the human condition. "The immediate effect of Columbus's exploits," Evans writes, "was to liberate the European imagination from the gloomy confines of its recent history, with the result that the idealistic impulse, which in the Middle Ages had been directed largely to the next world, could now be focused upon this one" (Evans 1979, 4).

The discovery of America not only required that maps of the world be redrawn, but that ideas about humankind be rethought and re-centered. As Evans argues, the New World was quickly invested with idealistic meaning by the leading intellectuals of Europe. It was paradise, utopia, a *tabula rasa*, a place of innocence, regeneration, and new beginnings. That it did not take long before the New World found its European detractors is beside the point. After Columbus, it was no longer possible to contemplate the human condition and its possibilities without taking America into account. Before America became a place to be fought over and plundered by the Old World and a destination for its emigrants, it was already an idea. The mythic significance of America to the elite classes preceded its practical significance on the world stage.

For the masses of Europe, however, the matter of the New World was rather different. Emigration on a significant scale did not begin before the early 1600s, and even then it was small compared to the huge migrations in the nineteenth and twentieth centuries. For these millions, the attraction of America had little to do with a philosophical idea of the place and more to do with a dream of opportunity, an exile from misfortune, or flight from religious persecution. What they knew about America, they learned from acquaintances or family who had emigrated, or who knew or had heard of someone who had. Or they may have learned of America through the advertisements of shipping companies. It is doubtful that many of the millions who emigrated did so because they had read and were inspired by accounts like St. Jean de Crèvecoeur's "What Is an American?" published in England in 1782 in *Letters from an American Farmer* and a year later in France. Crèvecoeur extolled the freedom, egalitarian spirit, and opportunities for material betterment and personal dignity that America offered Europe's masses. Likewise, Frances Trollope and Charles Dickens penned negative verdicts of the New World in the 1800s that probably had little impact beyond the members of the educated classes, many of whom had already formed certain prejudices against America. For the European elites, the idea of America tended to be associated with the human condition; for the masses, it was more likely to be associated with their personal condition.

Thus the beginning of an important and persistent gap arose between mass and elite perceptions of America at least three centuries ago, specifically in Europe. Almost no attention was paid to America in the Muslim world until the twentieth century, nor did the exploration, colonization, and development of America penetrate significantly the thinking of those in Asia or other parts of the world until the United States began to emerge as a global economic and military power at the end of the nineteenth century. Although there has been, as we will see, some evidence of an attitudinal gap between social classes in these other regions of the world, the situation for Europeans is different in a crucial way. For Europe—Western Europe, at any rate—the idea of America has always been connected to the European experience and European history. America was "discovered" by Europeans, colonized by them, and connected to the Old World by a complex and intimate web of language, religion, and culture. Consequently, while the idea and experience of America was a break from the Old World, it was also part of its history. From the time Europeans became conscious of America, their awareness and the ideas they held about it influenced their self-perception. Passionate views concerning America, both positive and negative, began to develop in Europe for historical reasons before they were found anywhere else. Likewise, the emergence of a rift between the perceptions of the masses and those of the elites began earlier in Europe than elsewhere.

"[W]ithout an image of America," Hannah Arendt observed, "no European colonist would even have crossed the ocean" (Arendt n.d., 410). That image, she argued, was never homogeneous across class and ideological lines. Historically, it tended to be sympathetic among the lower classes, for whom America represented the dream of opportunity and material betterment. The image of America was also positive among liberal and democratic thinkers, for whom America represented the promise of greater freedom and equality. But for the traditional European bourgeoisie, the aristocracy, and what might be described as anti-modernity intellectuals, America represented a sort of nightmare, the "evening land" of human civilization as D.H. Lawrence put it (1923).

Intellectuals write history, and the history they write has generally been that of the deeds and thoughts of the powerful and the privileged. And so we know much more about what European elites have thought about America than we do of the general population, at least in the age before public opinion surveys began to probe and measure the attitudes of the masses. It is possible, however, to infer the beliefs, hopes, and attitudes of the masses of Europe from the striking fact that millions of them left their homelands to start fresh in the New World. Among all the destinations they immigrated to, what would become the United States was by far the most popular. "God made America for the poor," wrote the British jurist A.V. Dicey in 1905, a sentiment that reflected the preponderance of both the propertyless and the unprivileged among those who immigrated to America. In the words of historian Robert Beverly in the eighteenth century, they were mainly "persons of low circumstances." Of course, one could logically argue that because more Europeans stayed home than left for America, the attractiveness of the New World may not have been so great in the eyes of the majority. In fact, however, the costs of emigrating and the sheer uncertainty about the future would have prevented many from contemplat-

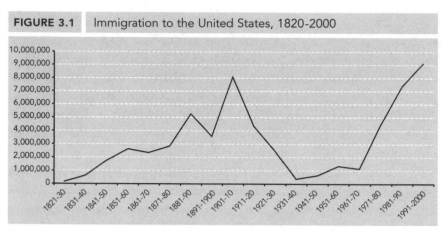

FIGURE 3.1   Immigration to the United States, 1820-2000

Source: United States Statistical Yearbook of the Immigration and Naturalization Service (2001).

ing the option, rather than any particular aversion to or negative perception of America. If exit is a reliable barometer of choice, as it surely is, then the flood of emigrants from European countries during the nineteenth and early twentieth centuries, and from a broader range of countries during the last half-century, must be interpreted as an indication that America has been viewed positively—more positively than the option of staying put—by the millions who immigrated to its shores.

Oral histories of families, literature, and the diaries and letters of those who made the decision to emigrate corroborate that America tended to be viewed by the Old World's masses as a dream of opportunity, freedom, and material betterment. That they were often disappointed with the reality of America, finding it harsher and less bountiful than in their hopes, is undeniable. This does not, however, diminish the power of the perceptions and motivations that brought them to America. Lebanese-born novelist Hanan al-Shayleh describes the aspirations and disappointments of her sister, who immigrated to the United States, this way:

> My sister used to picture herself disembarking from a passenger liner
> and being received by official welcomers, taken by the hand, patted on
> the shoulder, starting her new life in this model country warmed by
> their encouraging smiles. America was the land of dreams, stretching
> to infinity, resembling no other country on Earth. It had no antiquated
> laws. Its constitution was founded on equality and justice. Now she
> finds herself like a fish trapped in a net if she can't come up with some

collateral. But if she does find some, they'll drown her in debt. Debts will rain down on her from all sides, once she starts the ball rolling. (Granta 2002, 14)

These are sentiments that could certainly be expressed by millions, past and present. Despite this, Crèvecoeur's vision of America as a sort of everyman's paradise, where the dignity of social equality and the prospect of a better life for oneself and one's progeny could be realized, has been extremely tenacious.

By the 1940s, survey research began uncovering the beliefs and attitudes held by foreign populations toward the United States. In 1948–49, a major cross-national survey of the values held by the populations of nine countries, including how they viewed one another, was undertaken under the auspices of the United Nations Educational, Scientific, and Cultural Organization (UNESCO). This was, of course, just a few years after World War II and at the dawn of the bipolar world order that would exist for the next 50 years. Historical circumstances can be said to have colored the perceptions of America held by foreign populations at that time. How the world's populations see America has always been influenced, to a greater or lesser degree, by events that arise and then pass from the scene. It is particularly important to keep this in mind when big sweeping claims are made about changes in the world's opinion of America, as has often been the case since the 2000 election of the Bush administration and especially since the 2003 invasion of Iraq.

The image of America that emerged from the UNESCO survey, carried out more than a half-century ago under the direction of William Buchanan and Hadley Cantril, was overwhelmingly positive. Respondents were asked, "Which country in the world gives you the best chance of leading the kind of life you would like to lead?" Only in Australia and the United States did large majorities name their own country. Those who named a country other than their own were likely to name the United States as the nation that could give them the best chance to lead the kind of life they desired (see figure 3.2).

The state of postwar life and the still-raw memories of wartime devastation in several of the countries surveyed no doubt had a significant impact on respondents' satisfaction with opportunities in their home country. Moreover, the fact that the United States was chosen by more dissatisfied citizens than any other country was certainly influenced by the enormous

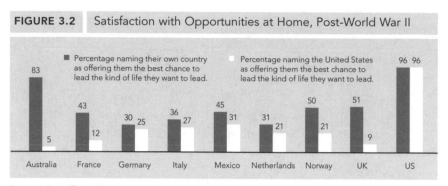

FIGURE 3.2   Satisfaction with Opportunities at Home, Post-World War II

Source: Adapted from William Buchanan and Hadley Cantril, *How Nations See Each Other* (Urbana, IL: University of Illinois Press, 1953), 30, 32.

gap that appeared to separate America's standard of living and international influence from those of other nations after World War II. But to dismiss the significance of the findings in the survey on the grounds that they are skewed by abnormal circumstances would be unreasonable. World War II and its devastation were part of the history of the twentieth century. They influenced, probably for a generation, how a number of national populations viewed their own countries and the United States. They do not, therefore, belong in the category of light and transient factors that sometimes influence public opinion any more than would the entire cold war era or the more recent period of unrivalled US dominance.

The attributes that the foreign populations in this study tended to ascribe to Americans were generally positive and were also, in most cases, quite different from the way they were inclined to see themselves. Table 3.1 shows the four adjectives most frequently chosen from a list of twelve as describing Americans and the four adjectives that national populations most often attributed to themselves.

With a few exceptions, the vast majority of traits most frequently attributed to Americans were positive. (Only Australians and Britons believed Americans to be conceited, and the French alone thought them domineering.) The terms *progressive* and *practical* were chosen most often to describe them. Interestingly, almost all national populations, including Americans, thought of themselves as peace loving and intelligent. These traits tended not to be among the leading attributes that foreign populations applied to Americans. In stark contrast to the favorable way Americans were viewed, negative terms predominated when respondents were asked about the attributes of Russians. "Domineering," "backward," and "cruel" were among the top four traits mentioned by all but one of the national populations.

At a more general and theoretical level, Buchanan and Cantril made a couple of important observations. First, the image that the members of one population have of another is more likely to be symptomatic of the nature of the historical relationship that has existed between these groups or their governments than a factor that has caused that relationship to be what it is (Buchanan and Cantril 1953, 57). Second, despite the often-heard claim that people can differentiate between what they perceive to be the attributes of a population and the character or behavior of its government, it is not in fact clear that this distinction is made by most people, most of the

TABLE 3.1	National Stereotypes: Words Most Often Chosen to Describe Americans and One's Own Population, Post-World War II*

PART A: Words Chosen to Describe Americans (in ranking order), by Country

AUSTRALIA	FRANCE	GERMANY	ITALY
Progressive	Practical	Progressive	Practical
Practical	Progressive	Generous	Generous
Intelligent	Domineering	Practical	Hardworking
Conceited	Hardworking	Intelligent	Intelligent

NETHERLANDS	NORWAY	UK	US
Practical	Hardworking	Progressive	Peace-loving
Progressive	Practical	Conceited	Generous
Hardworking	Progressive	Generous	Intelligent
Generous	Generous	Peace-loving	Progressive

PART B: Words Chosen to Describe One's Own Population (in ranking order), by Country

AUSTRALIA [1]	FRANCE [0]	GERMANY [1]	ITALY [2]
Peace-loving	Intelligent	Hardworking	Intelligent
Generous	Peace-loving	Intelligent	Hardworking
Brave	Generous	Brave	Brave
Intelligent	Brave	Practical	Generous

NETHERLANDS [3]	NORWAY [1]	UK [1]	
Peace-loving	Peace-loving	Peace-loving	
Hardworking	Hardworking	Brave	
Intelligent	Brave	Hardworking	
Progressive	Intelligent	Intelligent	

* Figures in brackets indicate the number of leading traits that a population attributes to itself that it also attributes to Americans.

Source: Adapted from William Buchanan and Hadley Cantril, *How Nations See Each Other* (Urbana, IL: University of Illinois Press, 1953), 51-52.

PLATE 3.1 Learning about America. In this photo taken in Brussels in 1954, schoolchildren are dressed as "red Indians" and sing songs that romanticize American history.

time. According to Buchanan and Cantril, "We recognize the distinction—when it is called to our attention—but it is not ordinarily an important distinction because whatever effect these people have on us is customarily transmitted through the entity called their government" (95). They qualify this generalization by saying that "the connection we see between [people and government] varies widely from nation to nation" (95). It is, of course, generally believed that the spike in anti-American sentiment that occurred leading up to and after the 2003 invasion of Iraq was in reaction to a *particular* American government and its *specific* policies, and may not have been accompanied by a fundamental shift in attitude toward the American people and other extra-governmental aspects of America. But, as Buchanan and Cantril observed, the mental boundary between people and their government is likely more porous than this belief suggests. Moreover, it hardly seems probable that a persistent and heavy barrage of negative information and images of a country's government and policies will not ultimately influence the picture others have of that country's people. The likelihood of this influence is probably greatest when the existing image held of a population is ambivalent and already includes significant negative elements.

This condition is certainly met in most countries. The image of America that foreign populations have held over the centuries has, at least in some populations, included negative elements whose influence on the overall perception of America and Americans could be magnified by circumstances. For example, Canadians—not only their cultural and state elites, but the general population—have long been resentful of America and expressed belief in their own moral and cultural superiority. Unbeknownst to most of the world, including America, Canadians are the world's oldest (but also least dangerous!) anti-Americans. At the same time, most Canadians have long thought of the United States as a friend and ally, and have long admired and sometimes envied, if often in a repressed way, much of what they see as American achievements and attributes. The negative elements in Canada's picture of America and Americans have become more prominent at various moments in history, when its relationship to the United States was placed under stress by circumstances that in the view of many threatened its interests or values. Examples include the Canadian national elections of 1878, 1911, and 1988, each of which hinged on the issue of greater economic integration with the US versus Canadian autonomy and national economic protection. A more recent illustration is the 2003 invasion of Iraq, when many Canadians were pulled in one direction by their close relationship to the United States and in another by a preference for a United Nations-sanctioned solution and cynicism about the Bush administration's motives, which was fairly widespread. In each of these cases, anti-American elites were able to exploit the negative elements already present in Canadians' beliefs about and dispositions toward America, creating a spike in the relative importance of these elements in the overall picture of America.

Contrariwise, events can generate a spike in the relative importance of the *positive* elements that exist in a national population's image of America. This certainly happened for many counties in the months immediately following the events of September 11, 2001. The case of France was probably typical. The elites of France have a long history of anti-Americanism. Not surprisingly, then, given the disposition of those who write and teach history in France, interpret current affairs for the French population, and dominate that country's national conversation, the general population in France also appears to have long held a less positive image of America than those of many other Western democracies. The UNESCO study carried out by Buchanan and

Cantril in the late forties found that among the Western populations surveyed, including Australians, Britons, the Dutch, Germans, Italians, and Norwegians, "friendliness" toward Americans, as measured by the researchers, was clearly lowest among the French (Buchanan and Cantril 1953, 54).

Nevertheless, the French image of America is a mix of positive and negative elements, as is true of virtually all Western societies. Surveys conducted for *Le Nouvel Observateur*, France's counterpart to *Time* or *Newsweek*, show that the French associate both positive and negative attributes with the United States, and also that the balance between these is quite variable over time. While the particular constellation of attributes that make up a nation's picture of Americans is probably fairly durable, the prominence of particular attributes and the balance between those that are positive and negative are more variable and subject to short-term influences. As table 3.2 shows, the United States experienced a net gain in sympathy and admiration among the French soon after 9/11. The speed with which both this sympathetic capital dissolved and the negative elements in the French image of America became ascendant is, of course, well known.

A downdraft in popular sympathy for and admiration of the United States occurred across most of the world during the period 2002–04. This was, of course, the period leading up to the invasion of Iraq and the subsequent tumultuous and violence-ridden occupation. But even as their image was taking a drubbing in matters of war and peace, a couple of major cross-national surveys showed that foreign admiration and positive sentiments remained strong toward particular elements in the constellation of factors that make up other nations' picture of America. A 2003 BBC/ICM survey of eleven countries, carried out when public opinion throughout most of the world was turning sharply against the looming invasion of Iraq, revealed that national populations continued to admire such aspects of America as its scientific and technological innovation, economic opportunities, and, to a lesser degree, its respect for freedom of expression and its democratic institutions. At the same time, some things about America were viewed much less positively. Figure 3.3 shows a mixed picture regarding the attributes of America that foreign populations thought other countries should aspire to achieve. Interestingly, while France emerged as the country whose people least admire America, seeing little there that should be emulated by others, Jordanians, who are overwhelmingly opposed to US foreign policy, tend to be great admirers of many American attributes.

| TABLE 3.2 | Rank Ordering of Words Most Often Associated with the United States, by the French (1988, 1996, 2000, 2001)* |

	OCT. 1988 %	RANK	OCT. 1996 %	RANK	MAY 2000 %	RANK	NOV. 2001 %	RANK
Power	56	1	57	2	66	2	57	1
Freedom	30	4	18	8	16	8	18	2
Wealth	31	3	27	5	39	5	27	2
Dynamism	32	2	26	6	34	6	26	4
Inequalities	25	7	45	3	49	3	45	4
Violence	28	5	59	1	67	1	59	6
Imperialism	12	9	21	7	23	7	21	7
Racism	27	6	39	4	42	4	39	8
Youthful	11	10	8	10	7	10	8	9
Naive	7	11	7	11	7	10	7	10
Generous	7	11	2	12	4	12	2	11
Moral Deterioration	15	8	13	9	14	9	13	12
No opinion	4	–	2	–	1	–	2	–

* Respondents were asked, "What words in this list do you associate most with the United States?" Total percentages exceed 100 because respondents could give more than one answer.

Source: Adapted from *Le Nouvel Observateur* (December 13–19, 2001; no. 1936), 58 (my translation).

The fact that very small minorities in all 10 countries surveyed viewed American popular culture as something that other countries should aspire to conceals the generally favorable sentiments expressed about American movies and music (but not television) by almost all of the national populations. Although only 2 per cent of the French said that American popular culture should be emulated, 66 per cent said they liked American movies and 55 per cent liked American popular music. Majorities—generally strong majorities—in 8 of the 10 countries said they liked American movies, and in 7 of the 10 countries clear majorities said they liked American popular music (BBC/ICM 2003). This corroborates the findings of the Pew Center's 2002 Global Attitudes Project, which found that majorities in 33 of 43 countries surveyed agreed that they liked American music, movies, and television. In fully 21 of these countries, including all the Western European and most of the Latin American countries, those who liked these American pop culture offerings outnumbered those who disliked them by at least a 2-to-1 ratio (Pew 2002a).

The Pew study found, as did the 2003 BBC survey, extremely high and widespread admiration for the technological and scientific accomplishments

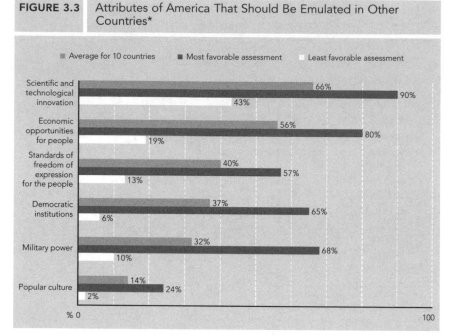

FIGURE 3.3 Attributes of America That Should Be Emulated in Other Countries*

* These countries are Australia, Brazil, Canada, France, Indonesia, Israel, Jordan, Korea, Russian, and the UK.

Source: Adapted from data reported by ICM Research, "What the World Thinks of America," prepared for the BBC (2003).

of the United States. Russia was the only country of the 43 surveyed in which a majority of the population did not agree that they admired the United States for its technological and scientific advances. Given the decline in their international prestige after the fall of the Soviet Union, a certain resentment among Russians toward their former cold war rival likely contributed to this result. In most countries, the proportion of the population expressing admiration for US technological and scientific innovation surpassed 70 per cent. This finding cut across regions and levels of national wealth, for example: Brazil, 78 per cent; China, 87 per cent; Great Britain, 77 per cent; Indonesia, 92 per cent; Italy, 79 per cent; Lebanon, 84 per cent; and Poland, 80 per cent (Pew 2002a). But while the world's national populations generally respect American know-how—an admiration whose long history is reflected in the observations of such early foreign visitors as Tocqueville and the Polish count Adam de Gurowski—they tend to reject the idea that American business practices should be copied. According to the 2003 BBC survey, more people said that the way America runs its economy should not be copied in their country than said it should. In most

FIGURE 3.4 National Attitudes toward American Ways of Doing Business (percentage who express a favorable view, 2002)

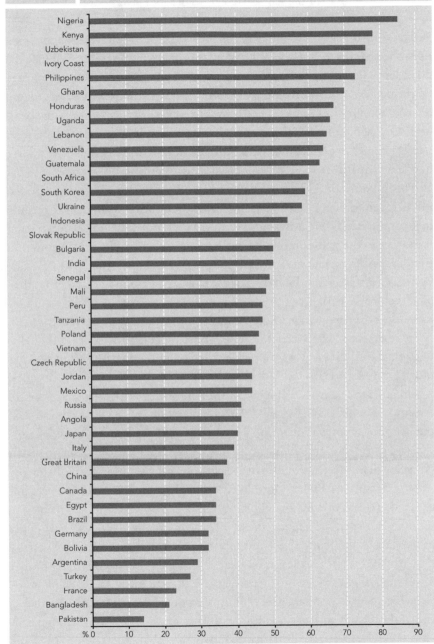

Source: Adapted from data reported by The Pew Research Center for the People and the Press, "What the World Thinks in 2002" (December 4, 2002), 68.

national cases, those opposed to copying America's economic ways out-numbered admirers of the American economic style by a ration of at least 2- or 3-to-1 (BBC/ICM 2003).

The danger of reading too much into a single question, worded in a par-ticular way and asked at a specific time, is brought home by the fact that the 2002 Pew Global Attitudes Project uncovered a somewhat different picture on the matter of foreign attitudes toward the American business style. Figure 3.4 shows a very mixed picture of reactions to American ways of doing busi-ness. On the whole, it appears that poorer countries are more likely than wealthier ones to admire this aspect of America, perhaps because the poorer ones associate the American business style with greater prosperity.

This mixture of admiration for and rejection of American ways is also found when foreign populations are asked about American ideas regarding democracy. The 2003 BBC survey found an enormous range in national responses to the question of whether American democratic institutions and standards of freedom of expression should be emulated. The 2002 Pew sur-vey posed a somewhat different question, asking respondents whether they liked or disliked American ideas about democracy. In 31 of the 41 coun-tries asked (Egyptian and Chinese sample populations were excluded), more people said they liked American ideas about democracy than said they dis-liked them. Admiration was lowest among predominantly Muslim popula-tions, Latin Americans, and Russians.

On at least one matter, however, foreign opinion of America appears to be almost unanimously negative. This involves the United States' impact on the distribution of wealth in the world. The 2002 Pew survey asked people whether they thought the policies of the United States increase the gap between rich and poor countries, lessen it, or have no effect. Even the Americans surveyed were more likely to express the view that their coun-try's policies exacerbated the global wealth gap (39 per cent) than to believe that they lessened the gap (22 per cent) or had no effect (25 per cent). Only in Africa and the Philippines were national populations more likely to say that American policies lessened the wealth gap. In the world's affluent democracies, the belief that American policies exploit the world's poor (which is probably a reasonable interpretation of the view that US policies widen the wealth gap) is so widespread as to be an almost unshakable con-sensus. Interestingly, the 2003 BBC study found that the populations of the wealthy countries were about as likely as the poorer ones to believe that

FIGURE 3.5   American Ideas About Democracy (percentage who express a favorable view, 2002)

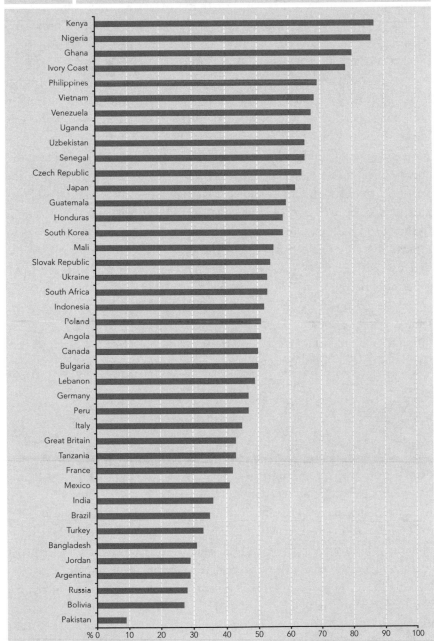

Source: Adapted from data reported by The Pew Research Center for the People and the Press, "What the World Thinks in 2002" (December 4, 2002), 64-65.

American economic policies made their own country poorer. Majorities in Australia, Canada, and France said that American policies made them poorer, a view that was echoed in Brazil, Indonesia, South Korea, and Russia. Only in the UK, Israel, and Jordan did more people think American policies made them richer than poorer (BBC/ICM 2003).

It is quite apparent that most national populations hold an ambivalent image of America. And while the particular configuration of elements in that image, including the balance between favorable and unfavorable impressions and beliefs, is extremely variable from country to country, a powerful reservoir of goodwill toward America exists and is able to withstand considerable battering. The Pew survey was undertaken after the post-9/11 bubble of international sympathy for the United States had burst and been replaced by a increasingly widespread belief that America's actions in the world had, to some significant degree, contributed to the terrorist attacks. Foreign media coverage of the invasion of Afghanistan and the detention of prisoners at Guantanamo Bay—an issue that received enormous attention in the European media, far beyond that paid to it in mainstream American—reinforced the generally negative foreign coverage of the United States on such matters as global warming and US refusal to sign the international landmines treaty or accept the authority of the International Criminal Court. Anti-Americanism was acquiring powerful momentum well before it became apparent that the Bush administration intended to force the issue of regime change in Saddam Hussein's Iraq.

In light of all this, the most surprising finding to emerge from the Pew and BBC surveys may have been the durability of many positive impressions of America. Even the BBC survey, carried out at a time of unprecedented worldwide protest against the war in Iraq, found that in most of the national populations surveyed more people said they felt favorable toward America than unfavorable. The Pew survey framed the question somewhat differently, asking people whether they had a favorable or unfavorable opinion of both the United States and Americans. This distinction seemed a reasonable one given the conventional view in the media and among intellectuals that foreign populations were less likely to blame the American people for those things they disliked about America than they were to blame the United States government. But the Pew survey found that in most countries the ratings for "Americans" and "the United States" were almost the same, usually varying by no more than 5 percentage points. In fact, in some Latin American countries, people were slightly more likely to express a favorable opinion of the United States than of Americans. Only in some of the predominantly Muslim countries were people significantly more likely to hold a favorable view of Americans than of the United States. Majorities—usually large—expressed a favorable opinion of both the United States and Americans in 35 of 42 countries (the questions were not asked in China) (Pew 2002a). These favorable impressions in most countries of the world, except some predominantly Muslim countries, persisted at a time when the question, "Why do people hate America?" was being pondered in newspapers, on television, and in books throughout the world.

The love-hate ambivalence that characterizes much foreign sentiment toward the United States is also evident in Muslim countries whose official relations with the United States have been, in recent years, strained or occasionally hostile. Surveys conducted for the Pew Global Attitudes Project in 2002-03 found that majorities in Turkey (53 per cent), Jordan (73 per cent), and Morocco (56 per cent), and a plurality in Pakistan (47 per cent) held unfavorable opinions of Americans. But in every one of these countries, respondents were likely to believe that their compatriots who immigrated to America had a better life now than they had had in their countries of origin (Pew 2004). And, interestingly, the populations of these predominantly Muslim countries were more likely than the Western European countries surveyed (France, Germany, Britain) to express the view that the world would be a more dangerous place if another country were as powerful as the United States (Pew 2004). Clearly, then, it is possible in the Muslim world to hold what might appear to be ambivalent and even contradictory views and sentiments toward America.

In a recent empirical analysis of this phenomenon of ambivalence in foreign perceptions of America, Giacomo Chiozza observed that "ambivalence emerges as respondents speak of America with two minds: appreciatively when they are induced to evoke some features and negatively when they are asked to focus on other aspects. Contradictory perceptions coexist in people's minds because America is an inherently multidimensional 'object' to which individuals relate in different manners" (Chiozza 2004, 48–49). Based on his study, Chiozza concluded that "Muslim respondents are not systematically opposed to all aspects of America.... The appreciation of American political and societal ideals coexists in the minds of the highly informed with the rejection of America's foreign policy choices in the

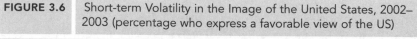

FIGURE 3.6 Short-term Volatility in the Image of the United States, 2002–2003 (percentage who express a favorable view of the US)

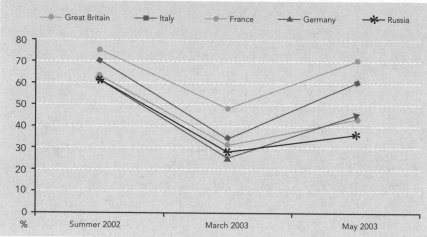

Source: Adapted from the Pew Center for the People and the Press, "War with Iraq Further Divides Global Publics" (2003), 19.

Middle Eastern political arena" (151). In Western European populations, Chiozza found that "even when [they] manifest their displeasure at the diplomatic posture of the George W. Bush administration ... they limit their criticism to the course of American policies while continuing to express warmer feelings toward the United States, as a polity and symbol" (152). The surge of anti-Americanism that swept across much of the world during the period between 2002 and 2004 hid from view this persistent ambivalence of world sentiment toward America.

There is, as indicated earlier in this chapter, an element of volatility in national attitudes toward the United States. This instability became very apparent in the spring of 2003, during and after the invasion of Iraq, when favorable ratings for the United States nosedived sharply from what they had been only a year earlier. Surveys conducted by the Pew Center during the spring of 2003 charted a steep decline in the percentage of Europeans having a favorable image of the United States, followed by a significant recovery in positive ratings a few months later. Figure 3.6 tracks this variability from the summer of 2002 to the late spring of 2003. Short-term swings of this amplitude alert us to the influence of specific events and media coverage on the image of the United States abroad. At the same time as the image of the United States was taking a battering, global views of

Americans remained quite positive in most countries, edging downward only slightly among some national populations (Pew 2003, 21).

The reservoir of goodwill toward and admiration of America, in much of the world at least, appears to be fairly strong and durable. Generalizations about the image of the United States abroad need to be qualified by the fact that ambivalence has long existed and continues to be characteristic of the sentiment toward America in many countries of the world.

CHAPTER FOUR

A VALUES GAP?

Those who have seen *Friday Night Lights,* a film about the Permian Panthers high school football team in Odessa, Texas, will recall that before and after each game the players gathered with their coach in a prayer circle. People who have gone to school in the United States and attended football or basketball games will find nothing exceptional in this. But a spectator from France or England witnessing this gathering would probably find it a bit unusual, and, on hearing that the team was engaged in group prayer, might even find it rather bizarre. On the other hand, this foreign spectator might find in this very American rite a confirmation of his or her view of the United States as a quaintly—or perhaps disturbingly—religious place. "Religious," in this context, means a traditional, old-fashioned, and rather backward place where abortion is still a political issue; same-sex marriage is extremely divisive; people believe in good and evil instead of striving to understand the complexity of human motivation and behavior; and the president is expected to make regular public reference to the Almighty and end every speech by saying "God bless America."

America is different. This conclusion has been drawn by foreign commentators from Alexis de Tocqueville almost two centuries age to Jean Baudrillard and Bernard Levi-Strauss today. The values and beliefs of Americans, most foreign observers conclude, are somewhat different from those of other societies, including those that are similar to theirs economically and socially and share the same Western heritage. Indeed, there is probably a no more frequent theme in foreign analyses of America than the putative cultural differences between the United States and other societies, and how these differences are reflected in social behavior, world views, and government policies.

Americans seem to share this conviction about their difference. Belief in
their own exceptionalism is as old as European settlement in the New
World. The line connecting John Winthrop's "shining city on a hill" to
America's vision of its place and even mission in the world today, as
expressed in any modern president's inaugural address, involves a faith in
the extraordinary character of America and the special role that Providence
has allotted to the United States and its people.

America is different, and in ways that interfere with mutual understanding between Americans and their leaders and the peoples and leaders of
other societies. The core values and beliefs of Americans are significantly
different from those of the French, Germans, Swedes, and even Canadians.
These cultural variations are not always very great and should be understood as differences in tendency—for example, the tendency to tolerate economic inequality or to believe that lack of religious faith makes a person
less qualified for public office—rather than the presence or absence of some
particular attribute. But in some cases the differences are quite sharp, and
their cumulative effect interferes with the ability of Americans and some
other national populations to understand each other.

For example, in 2003 the French parliament passed a law prohibiting the
wearing of the Muslim hijab in state schools. This law was passed by overwhelming majorities in both chambers of the French legislature and was
widely supported by the country's politicians and opinion leaders across the
ideological spectrum. In the United States, this law was generally seen as an
intolerant violation of minority rights and an indication that the French did
not have adequate respect for diversity. Viewed from an American angle and
within its prevailing understanding of minority rights and respect for diversity, it was not surprising that Americans would judge the French harshly.
But this was, nonetheless, an unfair judgment. France's political culture is
quite respectful of minority rights. Its Muslim minority, which constitutes
close to 10 per cent of its population, is an important part of French society,
and, despite occasional tensions and even violence, such as erupted in the
autumn of 2005, is not the target of official or systemic discrimination by
the state. France, like the United States, values the separation of church and
state. But the important difference between France and America, a difference that most Americans did not understand in the controversy over the
banning of religious head scarves from French schools, is that France has
become a very secular society in which official sanction of religious identities

that might be seen as challenging the French civic identity is simply not acceptable to most people. To put this a bit more simply, the dominant understanding of and debate over cultural pluralism is not identical in France and the United States. So it is quite wrong to suggest that the decision to ban head scarves shows that the French are culturally intolerant.

Misunderstanding works both ways. Since the time of Tocqueville, European observers of American politics have remarked on, and been critical of, what they believe to be the tendency of Americans to choose mediocre and even unintelligent leaders. James Bryce even devoted an entire chapter to the subject—"Why the Best Men Do Not Go into Politics"—in *The American Commonwealth*. In more recent times, European opinion leaders have shaken their heads over the popularity of Ronald Reagan and George W. Bush, asking how it is that Americans choose to elect leaders who, in their eyes, are so manifestly dull witted.

Of course, some Americans share their wonderment. But, without getting into the issue of whether these judgments are fair or not, I would argue that the longstanding tendency of many Europeans to be dismissive and derisive when it comes to the intelligence of American politicians is largely due to differing cultural expectations for and understanding of leadership qualities. This does not mean that Europeans tend to set the bar higher for their political leaders. The root of the difference lies in the populist tradition of America, where a perceived distance between leaders and those who elect them is quite often a serious liability. The influence of the populist tradition is highlighted in the disparity between the marketing of candidates in the United States and a country like France, and in the ingredients that contribute to an electorally successful image in these respective societies. I do no mean to suggest that those who would be president or prime minister in France, Germany, or Italy can afford to maintain an aloof and distant public persona, apart from and above the people. But there are differences between the sorts of personal attributes that tend to contribute to a politician's electability in America and those in other countries. When Ronald Reagan was asked the secret of his popularity with the American people, he answered, "When they look at me, they see themselves." It is hard to imagine Jacques Chirac, Silvio Berlusconi, or even Tony Blair giving the same answer.

Despite the fact that globalization has contributed to the undeniable convergence of lifestyles in many important ways, significant differences remain in the values and beliefs of societies that are otherwise quite similar in their level of economic development and the nature of their social institutions. In fact, it has become increasingly common in recent years to argue that the values gap between the United States and other rich Western democracies is growing wider. While this conclusion may not be warranted, there is little doubt that a gap between America and other affluent democracies continues to exist. This gap impedes the ability of those on either side to understand each other.

Drawing on data from the most recent round of the World Values Survey (WVS) (Inglehart, Basánez, et al. 2004), the chief dimensions of this values gap may be examined. Interestingly, these dimensions of difference remain the same as those that foreign observers have remarked on since Tocqueville visited America. They include the following:

- religion
- moral absolutism
- civic-mindedness
- individualism
- patriotism

In each of these dimensions, the values and beliefs of Americans are significantly different from those of people in other developed democracies. These are the differences that contribute to the wall of miscomprehension between Americans and these other societies.

RELIGION

Tocqueville argued that religion was a bulwark of American democracy in three principal ways. First, the plurality of denominations, none of whom was able to claim a majority of the population, encouraged religious groups in America to be respectful of diversity and vigilant about state interference with the rights of religious communities. Second, religion was crucial in preventing American individualism and materialism from fatally corroding a sense of community and corrupting the souls of men. Finally, he noted that most denominations in America were comparatively participatory and non-hierarchical, such that they acted as training grounds in democratic practice and norms.

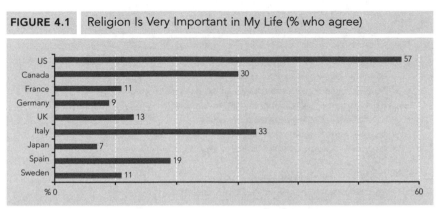

Source: Inglehart, Basánez, et al., *Human Values and Beliefs* (based on the 1999–2002 World Values Surveys).

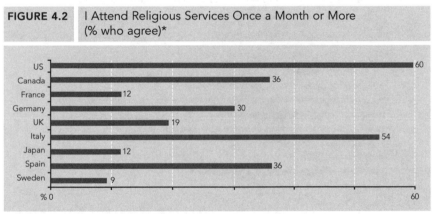

* Not including weddings, funerals, and christenings.

Source: Inglehart, Basánez, et al., *Human Values and Beliefs* (based on the 1999–2002 World Values Surveys).

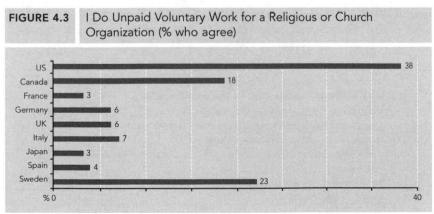

Source: Inglehart, Basánez, et al., *Human Values and Beliefs* (based on the 1999–2002 World Values Surveys).

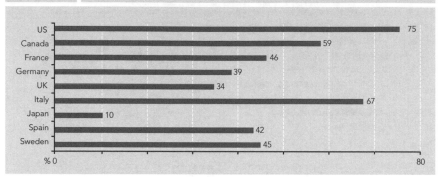

FIGURE 4.4 | I Have a Great Deal/Quite a Lot of Confidence in Churches (% who agree)

Source: Inglehart, Basáñez, et al., *Human Values and Beliefs* (based on the 1999–2002 World Values Surveys).

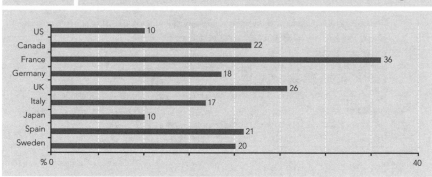

FIGURE 4.5 | I Agree That Marriage Is an Outdated Institution (% who agree)

Source: Inglehart, Basáñez, et al., *Human Values and Beliefs* (based on the 1999–2002 World Values Surveys).

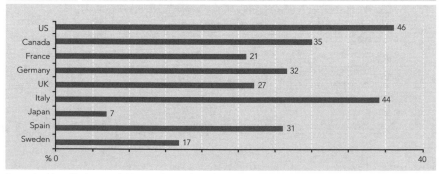

FIGURE 4.6 | Generally Speaking, I Think That Churches Are Giving Adequate Answers to the Social Problems Facing the Country Today (% who agree)

Source: Inglehart, Basáñez, et al., *Human Values and Beliefs* (based on the 1999–2002 World Values Surveys).

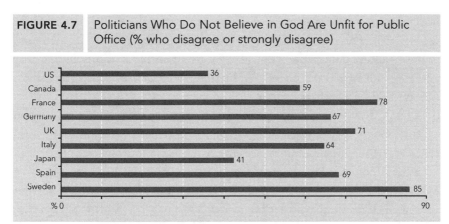

FIGURE 4.7 Politicians Who Do Not Believe in God Are Unfit for Public Office (% who disagree or strongly disagree)

Source: Inglehart, Basánez, et al., *Human Values and Beliefs* (based on the 1999–2002 World Values Surveys).

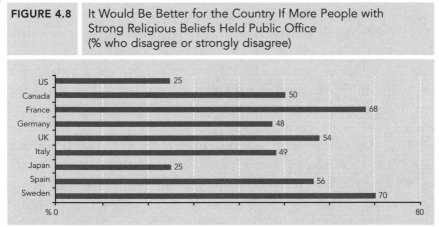

FIGURE 4.8 It Would Be Better for the Country If More People with Strong Religious Beliefs Held Public Office (% who disagree or strongly disagree)

Source: Inglehart, Basánez, et al., *Human Values and Beliefs* (based on the 1999–2002 World Values Surveys).

Religion continues to be important in the lives of many Americans and a factor in their country's politics. Today, however, most of the commentary on religion in America focuses on what is generally believed to be the much greater significance of religious values in America compared to other advanced postindustrial democracies. The evidence in support of this claim is overwhelming. And when people in such countries as France, Belgium, and Germany read about the influence of Christian evangelicals in politics, or hear the president invoke the Almighty several times in a single speech, or see on television thousands of anti-abortion demonstrators amassing in Washington, they find it one of the stranger aspects of life in America. They also tend to dismiss it as hypocritical, noting that this is the same society whose rates of divorce and crime are among the highest in the world, whose popular culture churns out vulgarity and irreligiousity at a prodigious rate, and whose leaders take actions and defend policies that fly in the face of the spiritual beliefs they claim to hold dear.

Hypocritical or not, there is no doubt that the role of traditional religion in American politics and culture is greater than in other Western democracies. Only Ireland and Italy have similar levels of church attendance. But even these countries trail considerably behind the United States on most measures of traditional religiousness. Figures 4.1 to 4.8 reveal that Americans consistently report behavior and express views on religion that set them clearly apart from the populations of other rich democracies.

When it comes to religion, it is plain that countries like France, Spain, and Sweden are on a very different wavelength from the United States. Americans are far more likely to believe that religion is an important part of their lives, to attend church regularly and volunteer their time to religious activities, and to express confidence in organized religion and its relevance to society's problems. They are also far more mistrustful of politicians who are non-believers and much more likely to think that it would be a good thing if more people with strong religious beliefs held public office. Many, if not most, Americans expect their president to make regular public avowals of faith. If the president of France were to behave in this way, most French citizens would think it inappropriate and many would believe such behavior to be dangerous. Any Borders or Barnes & Noble bookstore in the United States includes a section for "Christian fiction." This genre is almost unknown in the popular cultures of most other affluent democracies.

MORAL ABSOLUTES

European commentators will often remark that Americans are inclined to judge behavior and understand the world in overly simple, black and white terms. What Tocqueville and Bryce characterized as the idealism of Americans, Simone de Beauvoir interpreted as a sort of adolescent denial of the troubling disorder and complexity of the world. Americans, she wrote, are like "big children." "Their tragedy," Beauvoir argued, "is precisely that they are not children, that they have adult responsibilities, an adult existence, but they continue to cling to a ready-made, opaque universe, like that of childhood" (313).

When President George W. Bush described Iraq, Iran, and North Korea as an "axis of evil" and claimed that in the war on terror, countries had to decide whether they were *with* the United States or *against* them, foreign critics pointed to these comments as typical of what they believed to be a characteristically American tendency to understand complex circumstances in dichotomous, good-versus-bad terms. The president would regularly say that insurgents in Iraq wished to see the country return to "the darkness." His 2005 inaugural address was noteworthy for the moral clarity of his vision for spreading democracy, cast as the triumph of good.

Such language resonates powerfully in American public life. To some degree, it is linked to the continuing strength of traditional religious values in American society, as described previously. One would expect that those who are more frequent churchgoers, who have greater respect for the authority of religious leaders, and for whom religion is a more important part of their lives to be also more likely to believe that absolute standards of good and evil, of right and wrong, exist.

Although this tendency to understand circumstances and judge behavior in terms of moral absolutes cannot be dissociated from the religious tradition in America, religion itself does not provide the entire explanation. There runs through the public pronouncements of George Washington, Abraham Lincoln, T.R. Roosevelt, Franklin Delano Roosevelt, Ronald Reagan, and down to present-day leaders a conviction of the moral rightness of America, of its mission in the world and its role in world history. It is a conviction that, while often mentioned in the same breath as Providence, does not depend on religious faith. Rather, it is anchored to a sort of civic faith, what Lincoln called the civic religion of America. This "faith" involves the assumption that what Americans have aspired to create is, though imperfect in its execution, fundamentally right and good in its ideals. Jean Baudrillard captures this spirit of moral conviction when he says,

> The Americans are not wrong in their idyllic conviction that they are at the center of the world, the supreme power, the absolute model for everyone. And this conviction is not so much founded on natural resources, technologies, and arms, as on the miraculous premise of a utopia made reality, of a society which, with a directness we might

judge unbearable, is built on the idea that it is the realization of everything that others have dreamt of—justice, plenty, rule of law, wealth,
freedom: it knows this, it believes in it, and in the end, the others have
come to believe in it too. (Baudrillard 1988, 77)

Figures 4.9 to 4.11 show that Americans are considerably more likely
than people in other rich democracies to believe in sin, in the existence of
heaven (and hell, although these figures are not shown), and to agree that
clear guidelines exist about what is good and evil. When foreign commentators criticize the American government or the president for intransigence,
inflexibility, and unilateralism, part of the explanation may be that
Americans and their leaders are more likely than others to see the world
and particular issues in terms of morally good and bad choices.

CIVIC-MINDEDNESS

Tocqueville was struck by the propensity of mid-nineteenth century
Americans to join together in voluntary associations in order to achieve
communal goals. They did not wait, he observed, for the state to undertake
an endeavor that they saw as important to their well-being, nor did they
assume that such community enterprises ought to be the responsibility of
public authorities. Tocqueville believed that these voluntary associations
were the connective tissue of American democracy. They reminded citizens
in immediate and practical ways that they belonged to a community and
depended on one another. In doing so they helped overcome the alienating
tendency of the individualist ethos that was so strong in America. They also
contributed to what today's generation of commentators would call the
social capital of American society.

But this complex and vibrant web of voluntary associations made
another important contribution to American society: It created a particular sort of civic-mindedness that was centered around "we, the people,"
rather than the state. Part of what has been called American exceptionalism
can be attributed to the popular mistrust of government, a sentiment that is
often credited to the revolutionary origins of the United States. The historical propensity of Americans to come together in private associations to
achieve common objectives reinforced this mistrust and contributed to the

FIGURE 4.9 There Are Absolutely Clear Guidelines About What Is Good and Evil (% who agree)

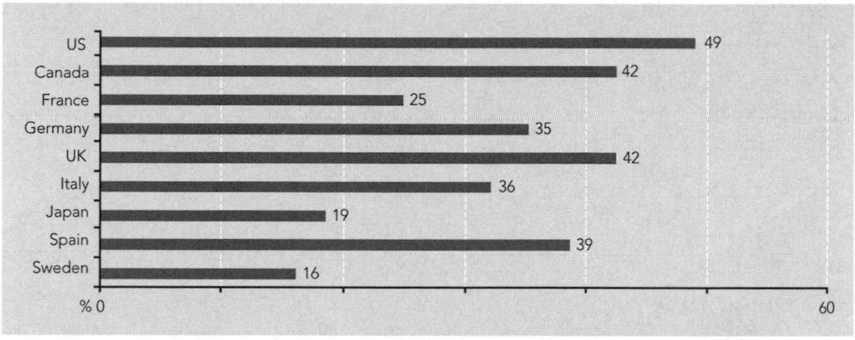

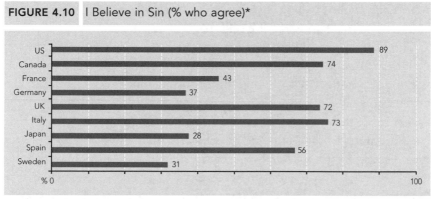

US 49
Canada 42
France 25
Germany 35
UK 42
Italy 36
Japan 19
Spain 39
Sweden 16
% 0
60

Source: Inglehart, Basánez, et al., *Human Values and Beliefs* (based on the 1999–2002 World Values Surveys).

FIGURE 4.10 I Believe in Sin (% who agree)*

US 89
Canada 74
France 43
Germany 37
UK 72
Italy 73
Japan 28
Spain 56
Sweden 31
% 0
100

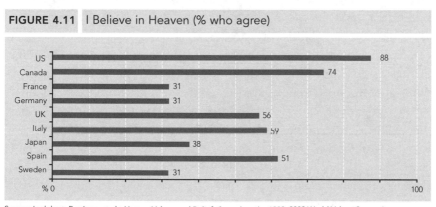

* This question was not asked in all of the World Values Survey (WVS) countries in 2000. The data reported here is for 1990.
Source: Inglehart, Basánez, et al., *Human Values and Beliefs* (based on the 1999–2002 World Values Surveys).

FIGURE 4.11 I Believe in Heaven (% who agree)

US 88
Canada 74
France 31
Germany 31
UK 56
Italy 59
Japan 38
Spain 51
Sweden 31
% 0
100

Source: Inglehart, Basánez, et al., *Human Values and Beliefs* (based on the 1999–2002 World Values Surveys).

idea that citizens *should* be responsible for organizing, financing, and executing many collective activities. More than a century after Tocqueville, Gabriel Almond and Sidney Verba argued that this was an important part of democratic citizenship in what they called the civic culture (1963). Citizens capable of working together to solve common problems and who saw this as an appropriate and important activity were more suited to democratic life than those who tended to view themselves as subjects, dependent on public authorities to organize their civic life.

Today, however, many people in America and abroad argue that the stock of social capital in the United States has been decreasing for years. Many go so far as to say that Americans actually have less of what constitutes social capital than do the populations of many other rich democracies. They point to greater spending on social programs and indications that Americans are less willing than people in these other societies to support and pay for a redistribution of wealth between segments of the population.

This debate over whether the connective tissue that joins citizens is weaker in America than in some other rich democracies often misses an important point related to the nature of American exceptionalism. The communal ethos that exists in America is less dependent on the state as the agency through which it is expressed and the instrument through which its goals are pursued than in other wealthy democracies. In fact, because of their historically grounded mistrust of the state, many Americans are dubious of government programs to achieve collective goals. The debate over faith-based delivery of social programs—a debate that is uniquely American—reflects this sense that social services and aid for the disadvantaged may be better provided by voluntary organizations than the state. It may be a mistake to conclude from America's lower per capita spending on social services that Americans care less than other populations about the communal goals that provide the ostensible justification for this spending. Perhaps, instead, they are more likely to place their faith and their dollars in non-state responses to social needs.

Data from the WVS demonstrates that Americans are far more likely than their counterparts in other societies to belong to voluntary associations and to participate in their activities. Figure 4.12 shows that a remarkably large share of the American population devotes some of its time to unpaid work for religious, youth, sports and recreation, educational, and cultural groups. In other rich democracies, these activities are more likely to be the responsi-

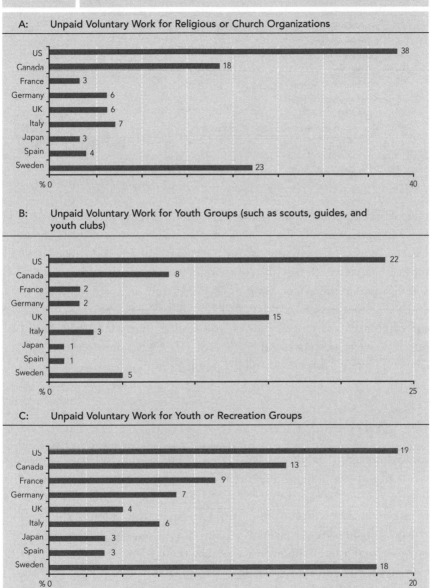

FIGURE 4.12 Measures of Social Capital (% who contribute unpaid voluntary work)

A: Unpaid Voluntary Work for Religious or Church Organizations

B: Unpaid Voluntary Work for Youth Groups (such as scouts, guides, and youth clubs)

C: Unpaid Voluntary Work for Youth or Recreation Groups

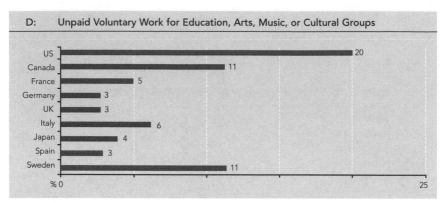

Source: Inglehart, Basánez, et al., *Human Values and Beliefs* (based on the 1999–2002 World Values Surveys).

bility of state agencies and financed by public revenues. If participation in voluntary organizations like these is a reasonable measure of social capital—citizens expressing their support for their communities and collective goals through voluntary efforts—then one would have to conclude that the level of social capital in the United States is comparatively high.

The fact that Americans are more likely to believe that private citizens and the voluntary associations they create—rather than the state—should be responsible for meeting social needs probably contributes to the misunderstanding between Americans and the populations of other rich democracies.

INDIVIDUALISM

Individualism is a concept with many dimensions. When Tocqueville wrote about the individualism that he saw in America, he had in mind what was then the rather novel idea that individual persons "owe nothing to any man, they expect nothing from any man; they acquire the habit of always considering themselves as standing alone, and they are apt to imagine that their whole destiny is in their own hands" (1840, 99). Commentators since Tocqueville have linked American individualism to such beliefs and attitudes as personal responsibility for success and failure in life, achievement orientation, and support for individual property rights and capitalism.

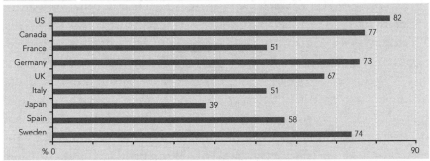

FIGURE 4.13 Feeling a Sense of Free Choice and Control over One's Life (% who agree that they have a great deal of choice and control)*

* The statement read, "Some people feel they have completely free choice and control over their lives, while other people feel that what they do has no real effect on what happens to them." Responses were gauged on a 10-point scale, ranging from the least freedom and control to the most. Those in the 7-to-10 range were considered to feel that they had a great deal of choice and control in their lives.

Source: Inglehart, Basánez, et al., *Human Values and Beliefs* (based on the 1999–2002 World Values Surveys).

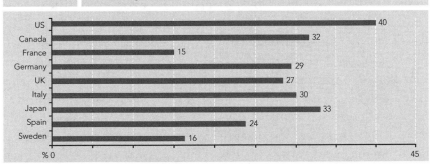

FIGURE 4.14 People Are in Need Because of Laziness or Lack of Willpower (% who agree)*

* This question was not asked in all of the WVS countries in 2000. The data reported here is for 1990.

Source: Inglehart, Basánez, et al., *Human Values and Beliefs* (based on the 1990 World Values Survey).

FIGURE 4.15 Competition Is Good (% who agree)*

US	71
Canada	70
France	46
Germany	66
UK	59
Italy	57
Japan	56
Spain	52
Sweden	45

% 0   80

* The statement read, "Competition is good. It stimulates people to work hard and develop new ideas."

Source: Inglehart, Basánez, et al., *Human Values and Beliefs* (based on the 1999–2002 World Values Surveys).

The evidence from survey research seems to support the claim that Americans are more attached to these dimensions of individualism than are citizens in other rich democracies. Figure 4.13 illustrates that Americans are more likely to feel they have free choice and control over their lives. When national populations were asked why some people are in need, Americans were more likely than others to point to individual laziness or lack of will power; in other words, to say that the person is to blame, not "society," "the system," "bad luck," or some other cause that is beyond individual control (see figure 4.14). One would expect a society that believes strongly in personal autonomy and individual responsibility for success or failure to be strongly supportive of competition as well. As figure 4.15 shows, the vast majority of Americans agree that competition is good and that it stimulates people to work hard and develop new ideas. Canadians and Swedes are about as likely to believe this, but skepticism about the virtue of competition is considerably greater in such societies as France, Italy, Japan, and Spain.

Individualism has always had an important economic dimension in the United States. When Harold Laski commented on what he called the American spirit, he stressed the faith that Americans placed in capitalism, private property, and free markets (1948). He also stressed the skepticism they expressed when it came to state regulation of property rights. This skepticism remains a significant point of difference between the United States and other rich capitalist democracies. Americans are considerably more likely to hold the view that owners should determine how their businesses are run, not the state or unions. Only Canadians come close to them in support for ownership rights (see figure 4.16).

Freedom is a slippery concept, but one that is obviously linked to individualism. The language of American public life—and, for that matter, commercial speech in America—is replete with references to freedom. Americans, it is sometimes argued, tend to understand freedom differently than do people in other democracies, being more likely to view it as the absence of constraint on individual choice and behavior. The populations of other rich democracies are more likely to believe that state action is necessary in order to provide the conditions for the meaningful exercise of individual freedom.

It appears that Americans are more likely than other national populations to choose freedom over equality when these values are presented in

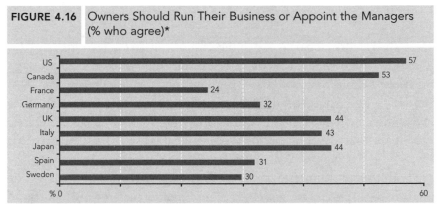

FIGURE 4.16 Owners Should Run Their Business or Appoint the Managers (% who agree)*

* The statement read, "There is a lot of discussion about how business and industry should be managed. Which of these four statements comes closest to your opinion?" One of the options was "Owners should run their business or appoint the managers."

Source: Inglehart, Basánez, et al., *Human Values and Beliefs* (based on the 1999–2002 World Values Surveys).

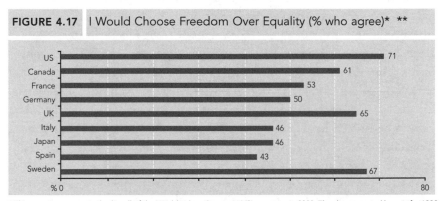

FIGURE 4.17 I Would Choose Freedom Over Equality (% who agree)* **

* This question was not asked in all of the World Values Survey (WVS) countries in 2000. The data reported here is for 1990.

** The question read, "Both freedom and equality are important, but if you were to choose one or the other, which of these two statements comes closest to your own opinion? a) personal freedom is more important; or b) equality is more important."

Source: Inglehart, Basánez, et al., *Human Values and Beliefs* (based on the 1990 World Values Survey).

conflict. Figure 4.17 shows that while the differences between Americans and Swedes or Britons are marginal, they are quite dramatic compared to the populations of France, Germany, Italy, Japan, and Spain.

PATRIOTISM

"Nothing is more embarrassing in the ordinary intercourse of life than this irritating patriotism of Americans." Tocqueville's words, many foreign observers would say, still have the ring of truth (1835, 244). Most Americans are very proud of their country and its ideals and accomplishments. Some commentators, both inside and outside the United States, ascribe this high level of patriotism to official and unofficial indoctrination—from reciting the pledge of allegiance each morning at school to the celebratory and triumphalist representations of America in much of the popular culture—and to ignorance of and indifference toward the rest of the world.

This was not, however, Tocqueville's explanation of American pride. He located the roots of their enthusiastic patriotism and what he characterized as their excessive sensitivity to foreign criticism in the democratic character of America. In today's language, one might say that Americans tend to have a sense of ownership when it comes to their society and its accomplishments. They do not see themselves as bystanders or pawns of forces beyond their control, but as shareholders in the great American enterprise. Consequently, they feel that its achievements are their achievements. And most Americans believe that these achievements, from the ideals and aspirations embodied in the Constitution to the standard of living they enjoy, are pretty impressive and deserving of pride.

For decades now, survey data have corroborated what one senses from the streetscapes, public language, and behavior of Americans. Figure 14.18 confirms that they *do* tend to be more patriotic and prouder of their country than the citizens of other rich democracies. Some may interpret this as an indication of "blind patriotism," a sentiment that may make Americans more likely than other democratic populations to support their government in military endeavors abroad. But, in fact, figure 14.18 also shows that Americans are not dramatically more likely than Canadians, Italians, or the French to say that they would be willing to fight for their country. This question was not asked of all the national samples in the 2000 WVS survey. But in 1990, Swedes were even more likely than Americans to express a willingness to fight for their country, and British respondents were only slightly less likely than Americans to express this sentiment.

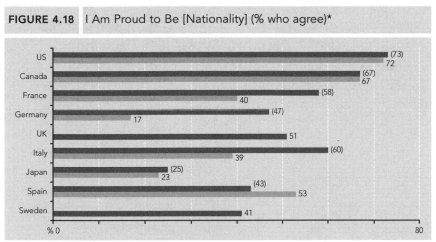

FIGURE 4.18 I Am Proud to Be [Nationality] (% who agree)*

US (73) / 72
Canada (67) / 67
France (58) / 40
Germany (47) / 17
UK 51
Italy (60) / 39
Japan (25) / 23
Spain (43) / 53
Sweden 41

% 0 — 80

* The lower bar represents the percentage of respondents who said yes to the question, "Of course, we all hope that there will not be another war, but if it were to come to that, would you be willing to fight for your country?" Sweden and the UK were not asked this question in the 2000 WVS.

Source: Inglehart, Basáñez, et al., *Human Values and Beliefs* (based on the 1999–2002 World Values Surveys).

CULTURE MATTERS

When trying to understand the ideas and sentiments that foreign populations have concerning the United States and its people, keep in mind that their values and beliefs are not identical to those of Americans. Sometimes this values gap produces serious miscomprehension, summed up in the exclamation of Georges Rémi Hergé's character Tintin: "Qu'ils sont fous, les Américains!"(Americans are crazy!). At a minimum, the gap contributes to a certain cultural distance between America and other societies. Colin Powell made this point during a 2004 visit to Europe, when he acknowledged that Americans needed to do a much better job understanding the values and points of view of other societies. But, he added, those other societies also need to see America more clearly and accurately, and not just through the prism of preconceived and sometimes unfounded beliefs and prejudices.

America *is* different. Most foreign commentators and leaders who interpret America to their populations accept this to be true. They know that culture matters and that American behavior, institutions, and policies cannot be explained solely by political interests. The quantity of books, articles, and documentaries devoted to exploring the values gap between

Americans and other national populations is enormous. Indeed, there is probably no theme that recurs as often in the mountain of foreign commentary on America. This important fact needs to be part of any explanation of why foreign populations react to America the way they do and why Americans and their leaders often seem perplexed by the world's assessment of them, their actions, and their motivations.

CHAPTER FIVE

ELITE PERCEPTIONS *of* AMERICA

When it comes to most things beyond the ambit of our direct experience, we rely on information from others to inform our impressions, images, knowledge, and, ultimately, judgements. As Walter Lippman said in *Public Opinion*, "The only feeling that anyone can have about an event that he does not experience is the feeling aroused by his mental image of that event" (Lippman 1922, 13). Those who shape and communicate the character of world events outside the immediate experience of most people play a crucial role in the formation of the public's perception of people, cultures, places, and conflicts abroad.

Although more people living in the world's affluent countries have traveled abroad than ever before, most non-Americans, aside from Canadians, have never set foot in the United States. The Pew Center's 2002 Global Attitudes Project found that about 9 out of 10 Canadians, most of whom live within 100 miles of the Canada-US border, had visited the United States. Forty per cent of the Britons surveyed claimed to have been to the United States, although this figure seems improbably high. The next countries, in order, were Mexico (27 per cent), Germany (25 per cent), Japan (25 per cent), Guatemala (24 per cent), France (14 per cent), and Italy (7 per cent). For most countries, however, the share of the population claiming to have visited the United States was in the low single digits, which indicates that only the elite strata have firsthand knowledge and experience upon which to base their image of America (Pew 2002a).

Through their influence on the media, foreign opinion leaders help shape the images and ideas that the general public has of American, its people, and its policies. However, as discovered in chapter 3, the beliefs and judgments about America held by mass publics are sometimes quite different from those of the intellectuals, opinion leaders, and politicians whose voices inevitably dominate the national conversation.

In this chapter, I will examine two issues relating to elite perceptions of America. First, what are the principal means through which information and images of America are communicated to elites and to the masses? Second, what impressions of America are conveyed to the public by foreign opinion leaders? The next chapter will assess various explanations for the beliefs and impressions held by foreign populations.

AMERICA THE BEGUILING

Historically, foreign elites have not always paid a great deal of attention to America. In the Muslim world, very little attention was paid to the United States before the middle of the twentieth century (Lewis 2002). In such parts of the world as China, India, Japan, and Africa, little was thought or written about America before it emerged as a world military power at the end of the nineteenth century. The first flexing of American authority in Latin America during the nineteenth century prompted the elites to think, speak, and write about the country that was emerging as their hemisphere's dominant power. In Europe, by contrast, it is not too much to say that the idea of America had an enormous influence on the thoughts and imaginations of Western elites since the voyages of Columbus.

Today, elites everywhere pay attention to America. Indeed, in some national cases, their interest appears to be an obsession. This is certainly true in France, where the idea of America has been important to how French elites understand their own society, the human condition, and world history since the time of Tocqueville, but particularly since Georges Duhamel's extremely critical portrayal of American civilization in *Amérique: scenes de la vie future* (1930), translated in English as *America: the Menace*. In recent years, the outpouring of analysis and reflection by the French on the United States has been staggering. While there is no denying that part of that spike in attention has been generated since the September 11, 2001, terrorist attacks, it is a mistake to imagine that France's preoccupation with America, well acknowledged by French commentators, is something that has only emerged during the last several years. As demonstrated recently (2002) by both Jean-François Revel in *L'Obsession anti-américaine: son fonctionnement, ses causes, ses inconse-*

quences (The Anti-American Obsession: Its Functions, Causes, and Consequences) and Philippe Roger in *L'Ennemi américain: genealogie de l'anti-américainisme français* (The American Enemy: A Genealogy of French Anti-Americanism) reflection and commentary on America by France's opinion leaders has been prodigious since World War II.

The same may be said for Great Britain's elites. The French may generate more words per capita about America than any other national population, with the possible exception of Canadians, but it is likely that the British devote proportionately more resources, possibly even in absolute terms, to studying, analyzing, and reporting on the United States. As of 2005, the BBC alone maintained a staff of over 50 specialized correspondents in the United States. When Hurricane Rita hit the Gulf Coast, the BBC sent a team of over 30 reporters, producers, cameramen, and technicians, easily the largest foreign media crew to cover that natural disaster. BBC America and BBC World devote much of their news and public affairs programming to the United States, and news programs on the main BBC, watched by Britons, include a heavy and regular dose of American coverage. The *Guardian*, Britain's answer to *The New York Times*, provides what is arguably the most extensive and highest-quality newspaper reportage on America outside of the United States. One need only peruse its archive of articles on America to appreciate the amount and depth of its coverage (www.guardianunlimited.co.uk). For example, over the four months from February 17 to June 18, 2004, the *Guardian* published 200 articles relating to the United States' election campaign. This was in addition to a large number of other stories about America, ranging from allegations of drug abuse among American athletes to the release and reception at Cannes of Michael Moore's film *Fahrenheit 9/11*. Even the tabloid papers, including the *Sun*, *Mirror*, and *Inquirer*, whose circulations are considerably greater than an upscale paper like the *Guardian*, pay considerable attention to the United States. The tabloid papers are distinguishable by their sensationalist front pages, and these often feature images associated with the United States.

France and Great Britain have extensive networks for American studies. These include professional associations of academics, journals, and university programs focused on various aspects of America, such as its culture, history, and politics. Britain probably has the most developed national network. The British Association of American Studies (BAAS) has well over

500 members (550, mainly in the United Kingdom, as of 2004) connected to universities and other organizations. In addition to BAAS's *Journal of American Studies*, several other UK-based reviews focus on America, including *49th Parallel, Comparative American Studies,* the *European Journal of American Culture,* and *Scope,* a journal devoted to American film. Roughly 40 undergraduate and graduate programs in American studies are offered at British universities. This adds up to a significant network of researchers, teachers, and students involved in the generation, interpretation, and communication of information about and images of America.

Institutionalized networks of American studies exist in many other countries, too. Some of the most developed can be found in Australia, Canada, France, and

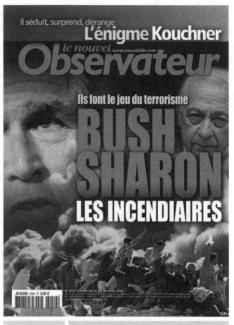

PLATE 5.1   "Playing the Terrorism Card: Bush, Sharon, the Arsonists." *Le Nouvel Observateur* is a French counterpart to *Time* or *Newsweek*. As may be seen from this April 2004 cover, the image of the US and its policies that is conveyed by mainstream media in France can be extremely negative. Reprinted with permission of *Le Nouvel Observateur.*

Germany, among others. Networks like these, composed chiefly of academics and researchers, constitute one of the principal ways through which the image of America is formed and re-formed within a nation's intellectual elite. Their influence does not, however, stop here. The media regularly turns to "America experts" for opinions on a story. Moreover, the teachings of Americanists will presumably influence to some degree the ideas of those who read their work or take their courses.

In this era of what George Ross has called "mass intellectuals"—the journalists, experts, television personalities, and popularizers who interpret the world to the general public—it makes sense to envision the process of generating and communicating ideas as a continuous band running from creator to consumer, passing through certain critically important distribution points. The creators include professors, researchers, writers, journalists, and other experts and opinion leaders whose activities involve interpretation. The information and images that they generate reach both attentive and less engaged segments of the public through various means, foremost of which are the education and media systems. These information systems vary dramatically between countries, from the totalitarian type characteristic of North Korea to the more competitive and liberal ones found in democratic countries. But the nature of the system is not the decisive factor in shaping the image of America.

THE AMERICAS PORTRAYED BY THE WORLD'S ELITES

There is, of course, no single or simple image of America held by opinion leaders from Paris to Karachi. There is, rather, an enormous range of images and beliefs, from the extremely hostile and critical to the sympathetic and admiring. Moreover, within particular countries, it is usual to find some diversity in elite perceptions of America, although the degree and practical significance of such diversity of thought is greater in Canada and the United Kingdom, for example, than in France and Egypt. (In Canada, for example, pro-American opinions are not so rare among opinion leaders. Consequently, policies and ideas that are supportive of the United States are likely to find defenders and receive a hearing in that country's public conversations. Pro-American sentiments are much more rare in France, where sympathy for American policies and ideas is likely to be interpreted as evidence of either an inferior intellect, gross ignorance, or wrongheaded ideology. Under these circumstances, dissenters from the generally anti-American orthodoxy have difficulty receiving a serious hearing.) It makes sense, therefore, to speak of the *Americas* portrayed by the world's elites, because there is no consensus among them on either the distinguishing attributes of America, the consequences of its actions, or its significance in world history.

Books like the best-selling *Why Do People Hate America?* give the impression that the thinking classes throughout the world are anti-American, and with good cause. This idea is not entirely true. It is fair to say, however, that opinion leaders in most countries—both those that are

usually thought of as allied to the United States and those whose governments and regimes are hostile—are critical of various aspects of America.
This stance generally pre-dates the end of the cold war and the emergence
of the United States as the world's unrivalled hyper-power. Exceptions can
be found, of course, and the balance between criticism and admiration
among a nation's opinion leaders and the stature of those whose voices are
pro-American varies between countries.

Despite the absence of a single image of America shared by foreign elites,
a dominant image crosses most national and cultural lines. Since the 1960s,
when the war in Vietnam and violence on the American home front created
a watershed in the foreign perception of America, the contours of this image
have included violence and aggression abroad.

AMERICA THE VIOLENT

Michael Moore's *Bowling for Columbine* was the movie of choice among
young Europeans in 2003. Moore's portrayal of gun culture in America,
and his argument that corporate and military interests are behind the culture of fear and violence that produces horrors like the Columbine killings,
found a deeply sympathetic audience in Europe.

Images portraying America as a society in which guns and gun-related
violence are woven into the fabric of life are so common outside the United
States, and analyses of this violence so frequent, that it is difficult to know
where to begin. At the extreme end, one finds representations like Swedish
animator Lief Zetterling's *The American Dream (Den Amerikans
Droomen)*, broadcast on Swedish national television in December 1976. It
portrayed the entire history of the United States, from Columbus to the late
twentieth century, as one of violent displacement, repression, and imperi-
alism. In 1993, to mark the twenty-fifth anniversary of Martin Luther
King's assassination, the BBC broadcast a fifty-minute documentary called
The Legacy of MLK. Much of the footage was devoted to scenes and
descriptions of race-based violence: the urban riots of the 1960s, the Los
Angeles riot of 1992, gang violence in South Central LA, and so on.
Viewers were shown a legacy of unabated violence between white and black
America. The Italian filmmaker Sergio Leone's classic film *The Good, The
Bad, and the Ugly* conveys a sense that amoral violence is deeply embed-

ded in the spirit and soul of the America that emerged in the West. Further examples of the ubiquitous image of America the violent are everywhere.

AGGRESSION ABROAD

The image of America as an imperialist power, intent on imposing its will and interests on others, is not recent. Canadians, Mexicans, and some other Latin American populations have believed this since the early- to mid-nineteenth century. The idea of America as a country whose political rulers, businesses, and popular culture industries wished to dominate the world became more widespread after World War II. Today, this belief is almost an article of faith among the elites of many countries.

Until the 1960s and America's escalating involvement in Vietnam, the view of the United States as an aggressive and imperialistic power was mainly held by two groups. One group was the Communist elites of the Soviet Union, its Eastern Bloc satellites, and China. The other group included left wing intellectuals in the West, chiefly in Europe. The image of America purveyed by the Communist group was based on the propaganda needs of states locked in ideological and geopolitical rivalry with the United States. The image developed and disseminated by the left wing group in the West was based on intellectual revulsion for what its holders perceived to be the genuine values and nature of America. A third but shorter-lived source of this oppressive image of the United States was the Nazi regime in Germany, which constructed a decadent and imperialistic picture of America for the purposes of propaganda.

Under Hitler in pre-war Germany and Stalin in the Soviet Union, the United States was already being portrayed as a country hostile to the interests and aspirations of these countries. State propaganda framed America as an aggressive power intent on world domination. (See the collection of German propaganda under Nazism and then under Communism in East Germany at <http://www.calvin.edu/academic/cas/gpa/>.)

The cold war rivalry between the United States and the Soviet Union reinforced this image of the United States as an aggressive and imperialistic threat. The portrayal of America and its international objectives by Soviet educators, the Soviet press, and official statements and documents of the Communist Party would have been unrecognizable to most Americans.

Shortly after the end of World War II and the partition of Germany into the Communist-controlled East and the pro-American West, a beetle infestation laid waste the potato harvest in East Germany. During this time, American planes were regularly flying to West Berlin, transporting supplies of various sorts to the population behind the Soviet blockade. According to the Communist authorities, the beetles that ravaged the potato fields and caused misery for everyone had been dropped from these American planes (see plate 5.2). Similar claims were made in 1951–52 by the People's Republic of China, North Korea, and the Soviet Union. Despite the fact that the historical record demonstrates that such charges were deliberate fabrications, many people continue to believe in them (see the Cold War International History Project at the Woodrow Wilson International Center for Scholars, <www.wwics.si.edu>).

PLATE 5.2   The Americans Did It! This poster from Communist East Germany in 1950 blames the United States for causing a beetle infestation that devastated the potato crop. Berlin: Amt fur Information der Regierung der DDR, 1950. Courtesy of Professor Randy Bytwerk, Calvin College.

Such stories, of course, sound absurd to most Americans, as did more recent pronouncements in 2004 by both the Castro regime in Cuba and the Kim Jong-il regime in North Korea to the effect that an American invasion was imminent. But from the standpoint of the image of America constructed and disseminated by the state propaganda machines of authoritarian regimes whose relationships to the United States are hostile, such stories make perfect sense. They serve the time-honored purpose of allowing for the mobilization of public opinion against the state's enemies, often deflecting attention from internal problems or even blaming them on a hostile foreign power.

After World War II, the intellectual left throughout much of the West subscribed to a broadly similar view of American actions and motives in the world, perceiving them as imperialistic and aggressive. The anti-Americanism characteristic of European elites, including the intelligentsia, prior to the war was not built around this image of America. It had been constructed around an image of America as culturally inferior and decadent, the "evening land" of human history, as D.H. Lawrence expressed it. The revulsion of European elites and the *réssentiment* they felt toward America was largely aesthetic. After the war, however, the notion that the United States was bent on world economic domination, and prepared to use all means necessary to achieve it, gained currency with the intellectual left. Evidence of CIA interventions abroad and the escalation and expansion of the Vietnam War into adjoining southeast Asian countries confirmed for these foreign opinion leaders the fundamental malevolence and selfishness of American intentions toward the rest of the world. In the mid-seventies, Simone de Beauvoir's argument that the United States was more reprehensible and a greater threat to mankind than Mao's China encapsulated the consensus of the European intellectual left.

In recent years, this image of America as an aggressive imperialistic power has become more widespread among foreign opinion leaders than ever before. Although there are some prominent dissenters, including such intellectuals as Ralf Dahrendorf, Roger Scruton, Michael Ignatieff, and Jean-François Revel, their voices are drowned out by the orthodox view held by most foreign thinkers. British playwright Harold Pinter expresses it perhaps more stridently than most when he says, "[America] is a fully fledged, award-winning, gold-plated monster. It has effectively declared war on the world. It knows only one language—bombs and death" (Granta 2002, 69).

Pinter's judgment on the aims and consequences of US policies abroad differs only in degree from much of the current conventional interpretation of American foreign policy in much of the world. On the occasion of the fiftieth anniversary of the World War II Allied invasion, the popular French weekly *Marianne* published a special issue on the "true history of the liberation." In response, one French reader wrote, "In fact, had Pearl Harbor not happened, Washington would have found another pretext to declare war on Berlin and Tokyo. This is because the US already saw itself as the new foremost world power and could not tolerate, in Europe or in Asia, the emergence of other pretenders to this status" (43). In *The Myth of the Good War* (2002), first published in 2000 in Dutch as *De mythe van de "goede oorlog"* and translated into German, Spanish, and French, Belgian-born historian Jacques Pauwels elaborates on this argument, squeezing virtually all American motivation and action surrounding World War II into a conspiratorial box of corporate, financial, military, and political interests. In

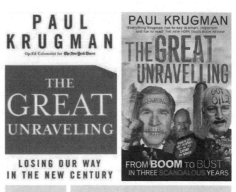

PLATE 5.3   The Great Unraveling. The cover on the left was used in the United States. The one on the right was used to market the book in Europe. Copyright © 2003 by Paul Krugman. Used by permission of W.W. Norton & Company, Inc.

the end, one is left with the sense that the chief difference between the nastiness of life under Nazi occupation and "liberation" into a world dominated by American capitalism is that the latter has proven more enduring and better capable of disguising its true character as it crushes the interests and aspirations of those whom it exploits. *The Myth of the Good War* was on the non-fiction bestseller lists in Europe for several months.

Jacques Pauwels's interpretation of the motives behind and consequences of American foreign policy is neither new nor particularly uncommon. Nor is it restricted to non-Americans. Noam Chomsky, Howard Zinn, C. Wright Mills, Michael Harrington, Michael Parenti, and others on the American left have made fundamentally the same case. What is new is the degree to which this highly critical view of American foreign policy has become the conventional wisdom in many countries outside the United States. This trend began during the Vietnam War, when people throughout the West— including, ultimately, many in the US—came to see this conflict as evidence of American imperialist designs and proof of the military-industrial complex that Dwight Eisenhower had warned about in his farewell address. But, today, with the end of the cold war and the emergence of the United States as the world's uncontested hyper-power, cynicism regarding American motives and reservations about a world dominated by the United States have peaked.

Consider, again, the case of European intellectuals. As we discussed, a tradition of anti-Americanism has long characterized much of the European intelligentsia. Historically, this represented an aesthetic and philosophical judgement on what they perceived to be the vulgar, culturally inferior attributes of America. These tropes still exist, but today's condemnation of America is more likely to rest on critiques of its actions abroad. For example, British director Ken Loach's contribution to the film *September 11*—a compilation of eleven short films made by directors from around the world, inspired by the attacks of September 11, 2001—focuses on the CIA's involvement in the overthrow of Salvador Allende's regime in Chile and provides a long list of ostensible American aggressions abroad. A similar list is included in Sardar and Wyn Davies's book *Why Do People Hate America?* (92–101). Germany's Nobel Prize-winning novelist Gunter Grass; Italy's Darius Fo, winner of the 1997 Nobel prize for literature; and British novelists Margaret Drabble, Doris Lessing, and Graham Greene: the list of powerfully anti-American voices among the European intelligentsia goes on and on.

For several years now, the immediate targets of criticism and anger have been the George W. Bush administration and American policies abroad, particularly in the Middle East. The widespread virulence of anti-Americanism among European intellectuals in recent years is, however, best understood as a spike in a general and deeply rooted antagonism toward the United States—its role in the world and what it signifies to them—rather than being a departure from a more America-friendly norm. There has been a wave of nostalgia among Europeans for the Clinton years, along with a pervasive belief that a John Kerry presidency would have brought an end to what they interpret to be the unilateralism, arrogance, and even perfidy of American foreign policy under George W. Bush. These sentiments certainly gave the impression that European anti-Americanism was a transient phenomenon linked to a particular American administration and its policies. This impression was mistaken.

There is, of course, a danger in speaking of European intellectuals in a way that implies they share a common set of beliefs when it comes to America. The same danger exists when one uses a shorthand label like the "Muslim perspective," the view from the "Arab Street," or when one imparts homogeneity of opinion or belief to any collectivity. Nevertheless, clearly the majority of Western European intellectuals, and the European opinion-leading class more generally, share a largely negative perception of the United States. This negativity has undoubtedly hardened since the collapse of the Soviet Union and the emergence of the United States as the world's sole superpower.

At the same time, European intellectual and opinion-leading classes admire what they perceive to be certain aspects of America. Not surprisingly, they are ascribing to America certain traits they believe to be characteristic of their own societies. In other words, "the America that we love" (L'Amérique qu'on aime)—the title of a 2004 issue of the French weekly *Le Nouvel Observateur*—is the America that looks like the idealized image European opinion leaders have of themselves. It is more collectivist, more statist, more egalitarian, more pacifist, and less capitalistic than the America that is the object of their contempt and criticism. An examination of this "other America" provides a good picture of what European opinion leaders admire about America and also, by contrast, what they abhor. "[This other America] is obviously anti-Bush. And even virulently anti-Bush," begins *Le Nouvel Observateur*'s survey of America. "But it is also creative, generous, and innovative. It is home to some of the most aggressive NGOs. It is a leader in literature and art, and at the cutting edge of both technology and ideas" (www.nouvelobs.com). The physical and spiritual center of this other America is New York City. Its voices include Noam Chomsky, Michael Moore, and Paul Krugman. The following were among those profiled in *Le Nouvel Observateur*'s survey:

HOWARD DEAN: Candidate for the Democrat presidential nomination at the time the article was written, Dean ran chiefly on an anti-war platform. He was described as "the symbol of the other America."

MICHAEL MOORE: Depicted as a fearless fighter for the underdog in America and the bane of the powerful, prepared to take on everyone from the president to such powerful interests as the National Rifle Association (NRA) and General Motors, his trenchant and merciless critiques of certain aspects of America resonate powerfully on the other side of the Atlantic. Moore's films and books, and the persona he has constructed and marketed, are commercially successful and politically influential in America. But his lofty status among Europeans as the foremost contemporary interpreter of America far surpasses his prestige in his home country.

JIM HIGHTOWER: The author of *Thieves in High Places*, he is admired for his theory that the United States has become perhaps the least democratic society in the Western world, a thesis that most Americans would be shocked to learn enjoys wide circulation among European intellectuals.

RALPH NADER: Activist and presidential candidate in three consecutive elections, Nader's argument that there is no significant difference between Democrats and Republicans, and his political idealism—similar in spirit to the European Greens and anti-globalization activists like José Bové—endear him to French and other European intellectuals.

NAOMI KLEIN: This Canadian and author of *No Logo* is described as being "a one hundred per cent citizen of the other America, the one that dreams of a better world and fights to achieve it."

PAUL KRUGMAN: Economist, writer for *The New York Times*, and author of *The Great Unraveling*, Krugman is celebrated for his role as a foremost critic of the Bush administration's economic policies.

CATHARINE MACKINNON: One of America's most prominent feminists, this law professor's longstanding battle to redefine and broaden the legal understanding of sexual harassment and address issues of sexual violence make her part of *Le Nouvel Observateur*'s "America that we love."

SEAN PENN: Actor and director Penn is well known as one of the most outspoken and politically active critics of America: the militaristic, imperialistic, conservative, capitalist-controlled culture that most European intellectuals agree has become the lamentable but authentic face of the world's foremost power.

*   *   *

Surveys on America like the one that appeared in *Le Nouvel Observateur* are quite common. For example, the Canadian newspaper *The Globe and Mail* ran a five-part series called Planet America in 2000. It started with a piece entitled "The Nation That Makes the World Go Round," in which the author, journalist Andrew Cohen, observed that the United States "is now so dominant that [the 2000] presidential vote is, in effect, a coronation of the king of the world" (Cohen 2000). In that same year, the conservative French paper *La Croix* published an extensive supplement called "Les Américains et nous" (Americans and Us), covering crime, mass consumption, inequality, diversity, religion, and more. Also around that time, France's prestigious *Le Monde* published a wide-ranging and generally critical supplement entitled "Voyage au coeur de l'empire" (Voyage to the Heart of Empire), produced in co-operation with *The New York Times*. British newspaper *The Guardian* regularly publishes in-depth analyses and commentaries on American politics and society. As we have seen, coverage and analyses of the United States—of both its domestic scene and activities abroad—has long been a staple of news and public affairs reporting across much of the world, in print and electronic media. The intensity of the world's gaze varies, but it never wavers.

On the whole, foreign coverage tends to be critical. This has not, it must be emphasized, only been the case since 9/11 and the war in Iraq, or under Republican administrations. It *is* fair to say, however, that the number and intensity of the attacks and negative interpretations of American society, culture, politics, and policies have reached almost unprecedented levels in recent years. However, if one goes back to the period from the late 1960s to the early 1970s, when the United States was mired in the Vietnam War, or even to the 1980s, when the Reagan administration adopted a policy of military buildup in its confrontations with the Soviet Union, foreign criticism was about as harsh and widespread it has been in recent years.

DISSENTING VOICES

Prominent voices of dissent, however, have always made themselves heard amidst the chorus of foreign criticism of America. Some of these voices are associated with particular national perspectives, such as those of the formerly Communist-controlled countries of Eastern Europe, while others represent ideological viewpoints of individual opinion leaders within national, ethnic, or religious communities. Each of the following cases illustrates dissenting, more pro-American points of view within a specific country or region.

Canada

Anti-Americanism is part of the Canadian soul, its origins going back to the American Revolution and the fateful decision by Britain's northern colonies to reject entreaties by the Thirteen Colonies to join them in declaring independence from imperial rule. But while most opinion leaders in English-speaking Canada have expressed the view that their society and political system are superior in important ways to those of the United States, this view has met with some significant dissent. In recent times, these voices have included novelist Mordecai Richler, who incurred the enmity of most of his fellow Canadian writers when he supported the Canada-US free trade agreement. He argued that those who produce culture ought to do so for the world, rather than depend on and hide behind the seductive protections that the state can offer. Similar sentiments have been expressed by Robert Fulford, one of Canada's leading cultural critics, who has characterized the virulence of contemporary European anti-Americanism as "almost Canadian in its odious condescension and ignorant resistance to fact" (Fulford 2003). Both Richler and Fulford likely would have agreed with Canadian filmmaker Norman Jewison, who has lamented what he believes to be the timidity and lack of entrepreneurial spirit in Canada's cultural community compared to that of the United States. "In the States," Jewison says, "people are dreamers. They dream the possibilities. Here, we're more likely to say, oh no, that can't be done" (CBC 1999). J.L. Granatstein, arguably English Canada's foremost contemporary historian, has characterized the anti-Americanism of English Canadian cultural and political elites (and, for much of the country's history, a good part of its business elite) as being both a cover behind which they could advance their own self-interest and a projection of their own insecurities (Granatstein 1997, 199).

Americans generally think of David Frum as a conservative journalist, author, and former speechwriter for President George W. Bush. Canadians, however, think of him as one of their own (born and raised in Toronto) and one of the most prominent conservative voices in Canada, where he regularly writes newspaper op-ed pieces and is a frequent commentator on radio and television. Frum takes a staunchly pro-American stance, defending the invasion of Iraq and castigating the Canadian government in power at the time for staying on the sidelines rather than following the example of Great Britain and Australia. There are other Canadian voices like Frum's, but there is little doubt that they constitute a minority within English Canada's mainly nationalist—which means anti-American—opinion-leading class.

France

No Western European country is more anti-American than France. This is true despite French protestations that, buried under certain American qualities—such as its Christian fundamentalism, its tendency to view world affairs in terms of good and evil, its retention of the death penalty, and its lowest common denominator "culture"—lies an America they like. French ambivalence toward America is longstanding and genuine. But so is French anti-Americanism (see box 5.1).

After the 2000 election of George W. Bush, French ambivalence receded and anti-Americanism was given full rein. But even then, and after the invasion of Iraq, some pro-American French voices would occasionally make themselves heard through the steady din of hostility and criticism produced by elites. Among the most prominent of these dissenters is Jean-François Revel, long one of France's most iconoclastic intellectuals. His recent book *L'Obsession anti-américaine* makes the case that French anti-Americanism, spearheaded by the country's intellectuals, "prevents us from seeing what really takes place in the United States and in the rest of the world" (Revel, quoted in *France-Amérique* 2004). While Jean-Paul Sartre, Simone de Beauvoir, Pierre Bourdieu, and others were dominating the French intellectual scene, Revel was one of the very few who maintained that the United States was the West's, and the world's, best hope for the protection of freedom and democracy. André Glucksman, another *vedette* in the French intellectual firmament, took a similar position during the Reagan years, arguing that "anti-Americanism now has the contours of classic anti-Semitism—power unseen; dark, violent forces beyond all control. The reproaches are the same.... The words are just different. 'They're everywhere. They are behind everything'" (quoted in Hollander 1992, 337). In recent years, it has become increasingly rare for any French opinion leader of significance to take something other than an anti-American line. Less than a year after the terrorist attacks of 9/11, the French writer Regis Debray published a book entitled *L'Edit de Caracalla ou plaidoyer pour des Etats-Unis d'Occident* (The Edict of Marcus Aurelius or the Case for the United States of the West), subsequently abridged and published in *Harper's* as "Nous

BOX 5.1 The Construction and Communication of an Image: the Case of Hergé's *Tintin en Amérique* (*Tintin in America*)

Belgian cartoonist Georges Rémi Hergé (1907–1983) was the creator of Tintin, the intrepid young journalist whose adventures have been translated into over 50 languages and read by millions of people, old and young. In the early 1990s, several of Tintin's adventures, including *Tintin in America* (1931), were made into videos and broadcast on French-language television in Europe and Canada, and later sold as videocassettes. Although Hergé's books have never experienced quite the same level of popularity in the English-speaking world, their top status as "BDs" (*bandes déssinées*, or graphic novels) in French-speaking countries is unrivalled. The 23 books chronicling Tintin's adventures have sold an estimated 180 million copies.

Hergé wrote *Tintin in America* before he had ever visited the United States. His idea of America was powerfully influenced by Georges Duhamel's *America: the Menace*, first published in French as *L'Amérique: scenes de la vie future.* This highly critical interpretation of America was popularized by French journalist Claude Blanchard in 1930 in a special issue of *Le Crapouillot*, a Paris-based illustrated magazine. Hergé was among the thousands of educated French speakers who read the magazine's riveting accounts and saw its dozens of images of life in America, including photos of a lynched black man, Chicago gangsters, cowboys, skyscrapers, vast open spaces, and, perhaps most importantly, images of mass society, conformity, and uniformity. Duhamel believed—and faithfully conveyed in the issue of *Le Crapouillot* devoted to "Les Américains"—that American civilization involved a way of life that crushed

human dignity and individuality, in both the automobile factories of Ford in Detroit and the dream factories of the Hollywood studios in California. America was, he argued, a society marked by extraordinary levels of criminal violence, stifling Puritanism, racism, crass and vulgar materialism, and a general lack of culture.

Much of this found its way into Hergé's *Tintin in America*. The picture Hergé painted of America was hardly more flattering than the extremely critical portrayal of the Soviet Union and the Communists in his earlier *Tintin in the Land of the Soviets* (1929). Although it would be a gross exaggeration to suggest that the image of America held by Hergé's millions of readers was determined by Tintin's adventures in the New World, it would also be a mistake to dismiss their impact. Hergé's memorable illustrations and fast-paced story reinforced certain ideas and stereotypes about the United States and its people advanced by writers like Duhamel. Moreover, Hergé influenced a mass audience when Tintin's adventures were disseminated via a medium—television, and later, videocassette—that helped burn his images and ideas of America deeply into the minds of fans. Interestingly, former French president Charles de Gaulle is reputed to have told one of his ministers that his only international rival was Tintin. (Hergé changed many of his ideas about America later in his life, after meeting Americans like Andy Warhol. But the deed was done. His image of America will forever be *Tintin in America*, which continues to sell tens of thousands of copies each year.)

sommes tous américains"—we are all Americans. Echoing the statement made by French President Jacques Chirac days after the terrorist attacks on the United States, Debray's book ostensibly argued that the best hope for protecting Western civilization lies in European countries accepting the inevitability and necessity of American global leadership. But the case was presented with a heavy overlay of irony, and the arguments framed as distasteful choices compelled by necessity. The spirit of Debray's "we are all Americans" could not seriously be considered anything but anti-American. Dominique Moisi, director of the French Institute of International Relations, took a more favorable view of the United States and its role in the world in the wake of 9/11. In a 2001 interview published in *Le Nouvel Observateur*, Moisi expressed a view that has become quite rare in France:

> Viewed over the long course of world history, I would argue that never before has a country had as much power as the United States and used it, on the whole, with such moderation. I would go even further to say that if the United States did not exist, it would have to be invented. The world would be infinitely more chaotic were it not for the United States. That America is far from perfect, we all agree.... But there is also an America that is indispensable, without which the history of humanity in the twentieth century would have been infinitely more tragic (Moisi 2001, 60 [*my translation*]).

French novelist Benoit Duteurtre reacted to the post-9/11 world in a somewhat different way, criticizing what he saw as the hypocrisy and insecurity lurking behind the anti-American orthodoxy that quickly swept away any sense of Franco-American solidarity following the terrorist attacks. "What worries me [about European anti-Americanism], " he wrote, "is certainly not that someone might criticize America, but that a pattern is emerging that is essentially nationalistic: one that entitles France, for instance ... to pass lofty judgements on Yankee power. It's as if, by adopting this stance, Europe hopes to disguise from itself the fact that it belongs to exactly the same world as America and is mired in identical contradictions" (Granta 2002, 32–33). Speaking of President Jacque Chirac's call for friendship and dialogue between Islam and the West, Duteurtre expresses a cynicism rarely heard in France: "I heard the inferiority complex of a Europe deprived of its role as a world leader ... but still quick to judge good and evil, while at the same time seeking to dissociate itself completely from the power—America—that has replaced it" (Granta 2002, 33–34).

During the period leading up to the 2003 invasion of Iraq, and the subsequent period of American-led occupation, sentiments like those expressed by Moisi and Duteurtre were almost never encountered in the French media. Among French opinion leaders, a near-universal consensus reigned that the American decision to invade Iraq justified the anti-Americanism that had long been the orthodox stance of French elites. Dissenting views simply were not taken seriously. When they did manage to surface, their impact on public opinion was negligible. For example, a documentary aired on French-language Belgian television just before the invasion of Iraq exposed the intricate and extensive web of French economic interest in Iraq under Saddam Hussein and how these interests would be jeopardized by the fall of his regime (Régie de télévision de Belgique français, 2003). These arguments, and others like them, did nothing to change the opinion of the French, and most of Europe, that the motives of its government in leading the opposition to the invasion of Iraq were untainted by economic and political self-interest, unlike the motives behind American activities.

Worse than being ignored, however, was the fate of French journalist Alain Hertoghe. His book *La guerre à outrances* (The War of Outrages), published after the American-led invasion of Iraq, examined what he argued was the systematic refusal of the French media to report any news of the war or provide any interpretations or images that portrayed the United States in anything but an unfavorable light. None of France's major newspapers, the targets of his charges of anti-American bias, interviewed him or reviewed his book. Hertoghe was fired by the conservative newspaper *La Croix,* where he was a deputy editor.

Countries of the Former Soviet Bloc

After experiencing two generations of Soviet anti-American propaganda, the citizens of the Soviet Union and its Eastern European satellites were left with very negative impressions of America and its government. The United States was, of course, the cold war adversary of Soviet Communism and was duly vilified by the official media organs of the Communist Party and in schools throughout the Soviet Bloc. There were, however, prominent dissenters, some of whom left the Soviet Union and its allied states in Eastern Europe to come to the United States.

Perhaps the most famous of these Soviet dissenters was the Russian writer Aleksandr Solzhenitsyn, author of *A Day in the Life of Ivan Denisovich* and *The Gulag Archipelago.* His 1978 commencement address at Harvard University was delivered at a time of intense national self-doubt:

America was still reeling from the experience of Vietnam and experiencing the turmoil of economic restructuring in a world with escalated energy prices and increasing competition from Western Europe and Japan. Solzhenitsyn told his audience that America alone had the moral stature and political might to challenge the spread of Communism. Moreover, he argued that it would be a tragedy for democracy and human freedom if, through an absence of will and muddled thinking on the part of America's elites, the country were to fail to perform this role. Solzhenitsyn's was an unconventional point of view almost certainly not shared, or only half-heartedly, by the Harvard professoriat gathered to hear his remarks. But, like many other intellectual dissenters from the Communist world, his perception of America and its role in the world was premised on the belief that life under Communism destroyed the dignity and freedom of the individual and corrupted the human soul. On another occasion, he confessed to being perplexed by the nature and intensity of the accusations leveled against America. "The United States," Solzhenitsyn said, "has long shown itself to be the most magnanimous, the most generous country in the world. Wherever there is a flood, an earthquake, a fire, a natural disaster, disease, who is the first to help? The United States …" (quoted in Hollander 1992, 336). In return, he went on, America receives reproaches, curses, denunciations, and even violent attacks on its symbols abroad.

Aleksa Djilas, son of the famous Yugoslav dissident Milovan Djilas, provides a straightforward explanation for the warmth that many Russian and East Bloc dissidents felt toward the United States: "The land of camps for political prisoners was America's beautician; its crimes and evil intentions made the wrinkles on America's face much less noticeable" (Granta 2002, 29). But if all that cold war dissidents saw in America was freedom from state oppression—already a pretty good deal—one would have to conclude that their positive sentiments only amounted to a belief that America was better than the alternative. In fact, many of these Russian and Eastern European intellectuals felt more than tepid approval of a country that did not ban their books or send them to state "hospitals" for the mentally deranged for expressing their political ideas. The Czech writer Ivan Klima, for example, recalls the impact that American cinema and literature had on him as a young adult and how the personal generosity of Americans and the civic freedoms he experienced in the United States deepened his affection for America (Granta 2002, 50–53).

The decision to invade Iraq in 2003 exposed a significant gulf between the feelings of Western Europeans and the citizens of formerly Communist Eastern Europe about the United States. Not only did Eastern European populations, led by Poles, express greater support for the American-led invasion, they were also more likely than Western Europeans to look favorably on a dominant American role in world affairs and admire American values and institutions. "Old" versus "New" Europe—with New Europe comprising the formerly Communist states—was how US Secretary of Defense Donald Rumsfeld framed it. The New Europe, he argued, was more sympathetic to American values and more in tune with the United States' view of how to maintain peace and stability in the world.

Pro-American feelings in Eastern Europe are rooted in gratitude toward Americans for supporting their thwarted aspirations during the cold war. But they are also fueled by skepticism and mistrust of the European Union, which most of their countries have joined in recent years, or at least by a certain idea of the EU that critics associate with domination by France and Germany. For these Euro-skeptics, the United States serves as an alternative to what they see as the bureaucratic, socialistic, and Franco-German dominated EU. In the Czech Republic, ideas and interpretations sympathetic to the United States find their way into the media because virtually all leading Czech newspapers are affiliated with major Western newspaper syndicates, and most of the columns they publish originate in the United States. This does not, of course, guarantee a sympathetic hearing for America in the Czech press; and, in fact, some papers, like the leftist *Pravo*, have been very critical of the war on terrorism and the decision to attack Iraq. Others, however, have taken a more pro-American line.

Britain

When asked which country is their best ally, more Americans name Britain than any other country. Most of these same Americans would be surprised to learn that anti-American popular sentiment ran almost as high in Britain during the invasion and occupation of Iraq as in other Western European countries, and, moreover, most of Britain's opinion-leading class has been anti-American since the Vietnam era. What Americans have seen in recent years is that the United States can generally count on the support and cooperation of the British government in military engagements abroad. No matter which parties are in power in Washington and London, this special relationship appears to hold true.

The partnership of George W. Bush and British Prime Minister Tony Blair after the attacks of September 11, 2001, and particularly during the invasion and subsequent occupation of Iraq, was emblematic of this special relationship and has deep roots. Its origins can, in fact, be traced back to Anglo-American cooperation in World War II. Today, however, this relationship is more usefully understood as a sympathy of ideas and interests that has been forged during the last generation as Britain has struggled with its connection to Europe, particularly the reality that the EU's center of gravity very clearly lies in France and Germany. Many British conservatives have remained skeptical or even hostile toward the powers and inclinations of the EU. They prefer, for example, the reality of close Anglo-American cooperation in military affairs to the idea of a common EU defense policy and coordinated military command. They tend to prefer the more pro-business and individualistic values associated with America to what they perceive as the statist and collectivist tendencies of the EU. Margaret Thatcher, British prime minister during the 1980s, was the classic embodiment of this pro-Americanism among British conservatives. It would be an error to interpret her preference for America or that of any other British conservative as simply, or even primarily, a consequence of Euro-skepticism. Doubts, however, about closer integrations into the EU leave the holders of such reservations with nowhere else to turn.

British voices sympathetic to the United States are many and prominent. They include some media outlets, such as *The Telegraph* and *The Spectator*. (One might also include the much larger circulation *Sun*, but the political content of that tabloid is often difficult to detect under the sports, celebrity gossip, and titillation that it serves its readers). They also find expression in the Conservative Party, although it has to be said that their voices have become fewer and less enthusiastic during the presidency of George W. Bush. Ideologically conservative think tanks like the Adam Smith Institute, the Institute of Economic Affairs, and the Centre for Policy Studies generate and disseminate ideas and analyses that are generally pro-American. Perhaps the most prominent English defender of a world that looks to America for leadership is the writer and philosopher Roger Scruton. In his book *The West and the Rest* (2002a), Scruton argues that "the attacks on America were a response to the world's most successful attempt at nation-building, which projects its power, its freedom, and its detritus so effectively around the globe" (2002b). The rejection by Western intellectuals of what they dismissively call the "Westphalian nation-state"—a label that calls to mind antiquated approaches to circumstances that belong to a distant time—and their embrace of transnational institutions like the European Union, the United Nations, and the International Criminal Court, are, Scruton argues, dangerous for individual freedom and democratic citizenship. He argues that the protection of rights and freedoms and democratic governance are necessarily linked to sovereign territorial states. The United States, he believes, has proven to be the most successful of these democratic nation-states and a far better hope for democracy than the UN or EU.

* * *

Although there are many individual exceptions to the rule, foreign elites have tended to portray America in a mainly negative light. Before the United States achieved the status of a military superpower during World War II, anti-Americanism was based mainly on a view of America as vulgar, decadent, culturally inferior, and soul destroying. Since World War II, the image of America as violent and unjust at home and aggressive and imperialistic abroad has become the main pillar of foreign elites' antipathy toward the United States.

CHAPTER SIX

What DRIVES ANTI-AMERICANISM?

An important fact is often lost from sight in all the discussion of anti-American sentiment throughout the world: *Most people in most parts of the world have a favorable impression of at least some aspects of America, if the evidence of opinion surveys, consumer decisions, and patterns of emigration are taken seriously.*

Ziauddin Sardar and Merryl Wyn Davies' book *Why Do People Hate America?* is profoundly misleading, the title alone seeming to imply that most foreigners hate America. Historically, European anti-Americanism was mainly the preserve of cultural and political elites, and, in fact, their sentiment rarely deserved the label "hatred." Contempt, distaste, and even repugnance more appropriately capture the anti-American feeling that has been widespread among European elites for centuries. Hatred more fairly describes the elite and mass anti-Americanism that existed in places like the former Soviet Union, the People's Republic of China before the economic reforms of the 1980s, and North Korea, past and present. In these countries, it was important for state authorities to vilify the United States through the official organs of propaganda as part of their efforts to maintain some level of legitimacy in the eyes of their own populations. Consequently, via state propaganda, the official hatred of America spread from the ruling elites to the masses.

But hatred does not quite describe most of the anti-Americanism that has undeniably escalated around the world in recent years, spiking around the time of the American-led invasion of Iraq. While hatred has certainly been directed at the Bush administration, individual leaders within that administration, and particular policies, vituperation has been alloyed by contrasting sentiments of admiration for certain aspects of America. Even in

Muslim countries, where anti-Americanism is generally thought to be greatest, the hatred that caused people to rejoice after 9/11 and when Americans
died in Iraq has been inspired chiefly by popular perceptions of American
policies, rather than the character and values of Americans themselves.
(That is one of the reasons why efforts by the US government to portray a
sympathetic image of Americans and their values through projects like the
2002 Shared Values television advertising campaign are largely a waste of
time and money.) Genuine and abiding hatred of America should be, one
might think, anchored more firmly in an unambivalent loathing of its
object. Instead, we generally find a mixed pattern of positive and negative
sentiments, even among some of the populations of the world usually
thought to be most hostile toward America. Authentic and durable hatred
toward the United States government and its policies, and American society,
values, institutions, and culture, does in fact exist in many parts of the
world. But this hatred resides chiefly among some elites, whose influence
on public opinion in their respective societies varies.

EXPLANATIONS FOR ANTI-AMERICANISM

In his book *Anti-Americanism*, Paul Hollander attempts to explain why foreign elites have so often expressed hatred of the United States, along
with milder forms of criticism. Drawing on Hollander, Andrei Markovits
emphasizes what he calls *réssentiment* in his analysis of anti-Americanism
among European elites (2003). Vladimir Shlapentokh ascribes the anti-
Americanism of contemporary Russian elites to their inability to acknowledge their own responsibility for the failures and problems of post-Soviet
Russia (2001). Bernard Lewis argues that the hatred of America found
among Islamist leaders, taught in the madrasas and exported abroad
through terrorism, is rooted in a deep and irreconcilable clash of fundamental values and beliefs (2002).

These are only some of the interpretations of anti-Americanism that have
been offered in recent years. An inventory of the main hypotheses,
expressed in the American voice, follows.

FIGURE 6.1 National Sentiment toward Americans by Real GDP per Capita

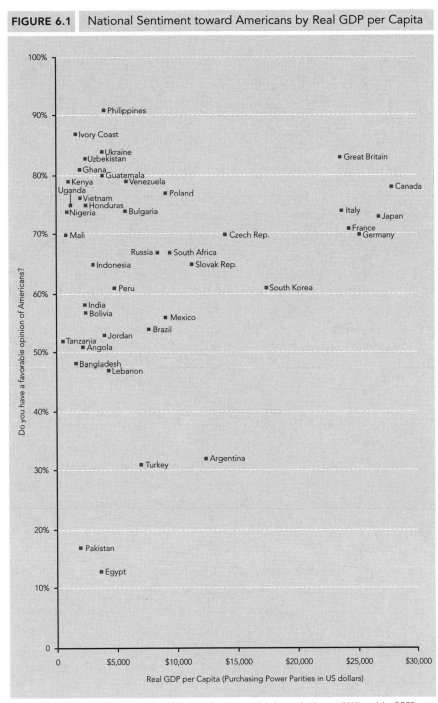

Source: Adapted from the Pew Center for the People and the Press, Global Attitudes Project (2002), and the OECD.

"THE MARGINALIZED OF THE WORLD RESENT US"

Turkish writer Orhan Pamuk uses the phrase "anger of the damned" to explain why, according to him, the attacks of 9/11 brought joy to many people on the "Arab street" (2001). His theory was echoed by the Italian writer Darius Fo, winner of the 1997 Nobel Prize in Literature, who said, "Regardless of who carried out the massacre [of 9/11], this violence is the legitimate daughter of the culture of violence, hunger, and inhumane exploitation" (2001). If one were to give formal expression to this hypothesis, it would sound like this: *If the levels of material deprivation and despair in a society are high, then negative sentiments toward the United States will also be high.*

This view is widely accepted among opinion leaders in both developed and developing countries. But the hypothesis is missing a crucial intervening step: The voices of the individuals and the institutions that blame America are the probable links between the misery experienced in a country and widespread anti-American sentiment among its general population. As illustrated in figure 6.1, poverty alone does not cause elevated levels of anti-Americanism. If a direct correlation between misery and anti-Americanism existed, one would expect to find most of the poorest countries of the world listed in the lower-left quadrant. In fact, there is no clearly discernible pattern in the relationship between the material well-being of a population and its sentiment toward the United States.

"THEY HATE OUR VALUES"

Another popular explanation for anti-Americanism maintains that it is caused by the collision of dramatically different, and perhaps irreconcilable, value systems between America and some populations of the world. This view may be expressed as a formal hypothesis: *If the difference between the core values and beliefs of Americans and another population is significant, then the likelihood* of that population viewing the United States and its people negatively is greater.

This hypothesis has two variants. One is associated with the writings of Samuel Huntington, Bernard Lewis, and Benjamin Barber. It focuses on the perceived gap that has existed between the core beliefs and social structures of the Western and Islamic worlds, and maintains that democracy has had a hard time taking root in predominantly Muslim countries because their belief systems are not especially receptive to the relationships, expectations, and behavior generally thought of as democratic.

A second variant focuses on what is believed to be an emerging gulf between the beliefs and values of America and those of Western European democracies, and is most closely associated with the work of Robert Kagan (2002). This thesis is less about clash of culture than about clash of value systems, implying that the gap—although politically significant and growing—is not so wide or historically rooted as a collision of core beliefs and social structures. In fact, considerable evidence exists that Americans tend to be more individualistic than their collectivist European counterparts, more religious in traditional ways, and more suspicious of state intervention (and so more sympathetic to market forces). Perhaps most importantly, Americans and their leaders are far more likely to believe that their nation has a special role to play and destiny in the world. Foreigners (and some domestic critics) often interpret this belief as sheer arrogance. Regardless, it is a vital and persistent strand that runs through the American cultural tapestry and has come to be taken for granted. This belief in national mission would be widely dismissed as delusional if expressed by a German, Briton, or Canadian but is assumed to be self-evident by many, if not most, Americans. Jean Baudrillard understands this difference when he contrasts the unconscious modernity of Americans—their unreflective confidence that they and their society are at the center of the contemporary world and the modern experience—to what he sees as the self-doubt, tentativeness, reflectiveness, and history-bound quality of European thought and behavior.

Ronald Inglehart and Pippa Norris have questioned the validity of the clash of cultures/value systems thesis, arguing that the main division between the West and the Islamic world is the place of women in society. The widespread acceptance of equality between the sexes and the equal participation of women in public life that characterize all Western societies today, including the United States, are not embraced in much of the Muslim world. They maintain that the real cultural divide "concerns gender equality and sexual liberalization. In other words, the values separating the two cultures have more to do with eros than demos" (Inglehart and Norris 2003, 69). This aside, they argue, the gap between Western and Muslim populations on the desirability of democratic institutions and freedom is not so great as to warrant the label "clash of cultures." Based on the results of the World Values Survey (WVS), Inglehart and Norris conclude that the populations of Islamic societies are about as likely as those in Western democracies to embrace democratic values and the institutions associated with them. But the measures used by the WVS to tap popular sentiment toward democratic performance, democratic ideals, and political leadership are quite abstract compared to those used to measure attitudes toward gender roles and morality. Inglehart and Norris seem to be aware of this problem, acknowledging that, "as heartening as these results [showing high levels of popular support for democracy in Muslim societies] may be, paying lip service to democracy does not necessarily prove that people genuinely support basic democratic norms.... [T]his sentiment needs to be complemented by deeper underlying attitudes, such as interpersonal trust and tolerance of unpopular groups" (Inglehart and Norris 2003, 70).

The WVS does, in fact, include measures of these core democratic values. If Inglehart and Norris had used these measures instead of relying on such arguably flabby response items as "Democracy may have problems, but it's better than any other form of government," they may have concluded that the cultural divide between the West and the Islamic world is quite wide. For example, respondents in all countries were asked by the WVS to consider various types of political systems and think about each as a way of governing their country. The statement "Having a strong leader who does not have to bother with parliament and elections"—quite obviously undemocratic—was described as either fairly or very good by 47 per cent of the population in a sample of four Muslin countries (Iran, Jordan, Pakistan, and Turkey). Only 28 per cent of respondents agreed with the statement in a sample of four Western democracies (Canada, France, Great Britain, the United States). As to whether they would dislike having someone of another race as a neighbor, respondents from the sample of four Muslim countries were three times more likely than those from the four Western democracies to agree with this statement (Inglehart, Basánez, et al. 2004). It seems clear, therefore, that the cultural divide between the West and the Islamic world when it comes to democracy is not as narrow as Inglehart and Norris suggest.

"DEMOCRACIES WILL LIKE US"

Spokespersons for the United States government and conservative opinion leaders often suggest that as societies and their governments become more democratic, they will also come to view America more favorably. Formal hypothesis: *If a society has well-established and stable democratic structures and values, then it is likely to be favorably disposed toward America and have a positive view of its politics.* This is obviously a variation on the clash of cultures thesis. It is based on the premise that similarity in political characteristics should generate affective sympathy, and dissimilarity will reduce the likelihood of identification and admiration. In other words, a political system that is seen to embody radically different principles and practices is likely to produce feelings of alienation.

But according to measures provided by Freedom House (a non-partisan organization founded over sixty years ago by Eleanor Roosevelt with the mission of monitoring and promoting the spread of democracy throughout the world) there is no clear pattern of correspondence between whether a country is more or less democratic and its sentiment toward the United States (see figure 6.2). Several well-established democracies, including France, Belgium, Germany, and Canada, score higher on the anti-Americanism index than many countries Freedom House characterizes as "not free" or "partly free," some of whom do not even hold elections.

"FREEDOM OF THE PRESS WILL ENABLE THE WORLD'S POPULATIONS TO SEE US AS WE TRULY ARE"

According to this line of reasoning, much of the anti-Americanism that exists throughout the world has been caused by distorted images and false or biased information about the United States communicated through national media systems controlled by regimes hostile to America. There is, of course, considerable truth in the claim that the propaganda machines of some regimes—such as the former Soviet Union, the People's Republic of China before its enthusiastic entry into the world capitalist economy, and present-day North Korea and Cuba—have generated a steady diet of anti-American information for domestic consumption. It is also true that access to alternative sources of information in these regimes is limited. It seems

FIGURE 6.2 National Sentiment toward Americans by Degree of Democracy

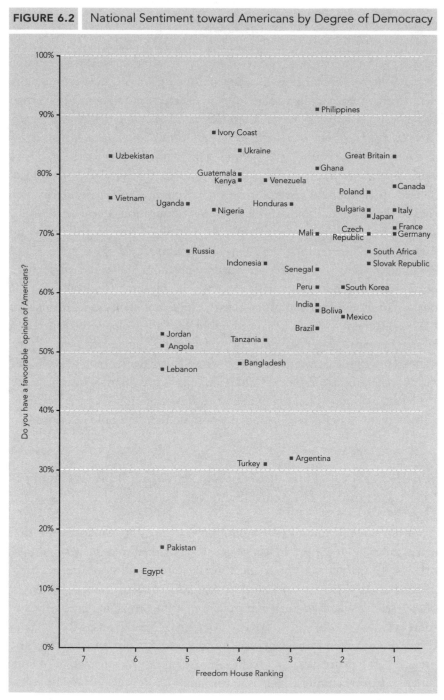

Source: Adapted from the Pew Center for the People and the Press, Global Attitudes Project (2002), and the OECD.

reasonable to expect that a country with a state monopoly media system will be profoundly undemocratic in other respects and more likely to convey a negative image of the United States and its policies. Stated as a formal hypothesis, this argument would take the following form: *If a population has relatively unrestricted access to a variety of sources of information, including film, television, news reporting, the Internet, and books, then it is more likely to have a positive impression of America.*

During the cold war, the US State Department invested significant resources trying to reach the populations of Soviet Bloc countries with radio programming from the West. Radio Free Europe and the Voice of America were the most prominent examples of this campaign to counter anti-American state propaganda. How effective their measures were is open to argument, but it is doubtful they played more than a marginal role in the demise of Soviet Communism. Regardless, the State Department continues to embrace the assumption that "to know us is to love us (or at least to not hate us!)." In order to counter the heavy and steady anti-Americanism purveyed by al-Jazeera and other Arab broadcasters, and to generate a more sympathetic image of the United States in the Muslim world, the State Department has helped launch radio and television broadcasts to Arab communities abroad and at home. Radio Sawa, which replaced the Arab-language Voice of America in the Middle East, is funded by the State Department and broadcasts pop music and news. It has been joined by Radio Farda, a 24-hour broadcaster that offers a mix of news and entertainment. The US State Department also helps finance *Hi*, a glossy Arab-language magazine that focuses on Arab-American life. It was also responsible for the Shared Values campaign launched in 2002, when anti-American sentiment throughout the Muslim world was spiking. The short television ads in the campaign showed Muslim Americans in various roles and communities across the United States—business owners, a teacher, a firefighter, a university student, a prominent medical researcher—who were able to practice their religion, maintain their values, and be accepted by their non-Muslim neighbors. They were broadcast on television in several Muslim countries, but some stations flat out refused to carry them.

Changes in technology have made it more difficult for repressive regimes to police their information borders, so the number of national media systems that are effectively closed to outside information and points of view has been reduced. However, significant national differences in the freedom of the media continue to exist. Using Freedom House's measurements of press freedom, which are based chiefly on the structure of news-delivery systems and the influence of laws and administrative regulations on the content of print and broadcast media, I have organized the world's countries along a scale ranging from those with the freest to the least-free media systems. Freedom House's measures do not enable us to know how porous a country's information borders are or how widespread popular consumption of news and other outside information is. Nevertheless, if we accept its measures as a reasonably reliable indication of a population's access to a variety of information sources, then it does not appear that a freer media system correlates strongly with more positive sentiments toward the United States.

"THOSE WE HAVE HARMED WILL RESENT US, AND THOSE WE HAVE AIDED WILL APPRECIATE US"

It seems quite plausible that a population's view of the United States will be influenced by the actual relations that have existed between the two counties. One would expect to find that the countries that have hostile relations with the United States, and whose opinion leaders will certainly have painted a negative picture on these grounds, will be less favorably disposed than those whose relations with America are not marked by hostility. Formal hypothesis: *If the official government-to-government relations between the United States and another country are characterized by persistent or serious hostility, then the likelihood is greater that the country's population will have a negative perception of America.*

Much of the recent literature on anti-Americanism, particularly anti-Americanism in the Muslin world, assumes the validity of this hypothesis. The late Edward Said is probably the best-known exponent of this view. According to Said, American policies that favor Israeli territorial claims and security interests over those of the Palestinians are the fundamental cause of anti-Americanism in the Arab Muslim world and in Muslim countries outside the Middle East. He insisted that policy differences, not cultural differences, are the basis for Muslim anti-Americanism. This view is also expressed by Sardar and Wynn Davies in *Why Do People Hate America?* and by many, if not most, commentators on America's relations with the

FIGURE 6.3 National Sentiment toward Americans by Degree of Press Freedom

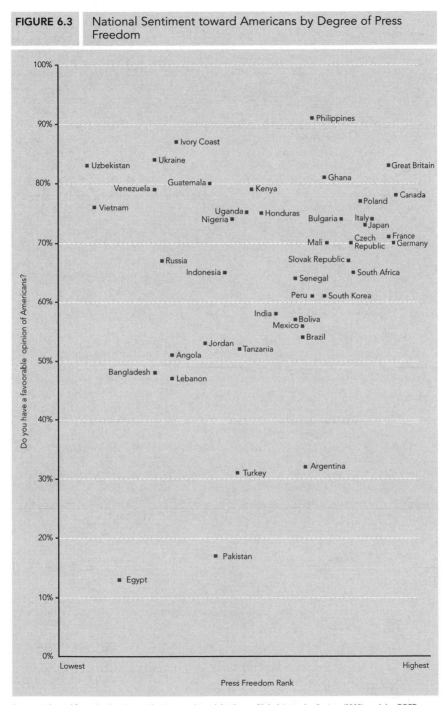

Source: Adapted from the Pew Center for the People and the Press, Global Attitudes Project (2002), and the OECD.

BOX 6.1 Al-Jazeera's Competition

As important as al-Jazeera has been in promoting a sense of unity and *ummah*, it does not have the television field all to itself. Al-Arabiya, a Saudi-owned 24-hour news channel based in Dubai, was launched in 2003 as a direct competitor to al-Jazeera. Owned by a brother-in-law of Saudi Arabia's King Fahd, al-Arabiya has taken a generally pro-American line in its coverage of Iraq since 2004. "We attract liberal-minded people," says Abdul Rahman al-Rashed, al-Arabiya's chief editor (*Economist* 2005). Viewership surveys in 2005 found that more Iraqis watched al-Arabiya than al-Jazeera, and the two broadcasters were about equally popular in Saudi Arabia. In Egypt, however, al-Jazeera was considerably more popular, with twice as many people claiming to watch it regularly than those who tuned into al-Arabiya on a regular basis.

Al-Arabiya has a couple of additional advantages over its Qatar-based rival. One is money. Al-Arabiya is part of a larger broadcasting company that includes two of the Middle East's most profitable commercial channels. Al-Jazeera's finances are much more precarious, and, in 2005, the government of Qatar indicated its intention to privatize the channel. The other advantage is that al-Arabiya has greater access to newsmakers and the places where news is being made. Al-Jazeera built its reputation and influence in the Arab and Muslim worlds with its coverage of the Palestinian *intifada* that began in October 2000, followed by its graphic coverage of the war in Iraq. It won the attention of the West when

it became Osama bin Laden's channel of choice for disseminating his occasional video messages after 9/11, and for airing video footage of hostages held and killed by insurgents in Iraq. Al-Jazeera came to be seen by many in the Arab world and elsewhere as representing the Sunni Muslim, Arab nationalist view that armed resistance to infidel occupation is always legitimate and noble. Many of its viewers doubtless agree. But al-Jazeera crews have been banned from Iraq, Kuwait, Bahrain, and Saudi Arabia because of this sort of coverage.

Al-Jazeera and al-Arabiya are the two giants of the Arab news world, but they have no monopoly on the market. The US State Department launched al-Hurra in 2005, which broadcasts in Arabic from Washington. According to most accounts, however, al-Hurra has not made serious inroads into the Arab television news market, perhaps because its objectivity is seen to be dubious. At the other end of the spectrum is al-Manar, a satellite channel run by Hizbullah, which is very popular among Palestinians. (Americans with satellite television can see how news from the Middle East is covered by broadcasters in that region by watching Link TV <www.linktv.org>, a non-profit satellite channel operated out of California. Its *Mosaic: World News from the Middle East* provides a daily selection of news stories from broadcasters in such countries as Iran, the United Arab Emirates, and Egypt, dubbed into English.)

Arab countries of the Middle East and the wider Muslim world (Waterbury 2003; Pintak 2003).

This hostile relations hypothesis can be applied to the Muslim world as a whole, in addition to particular countries. It is not necessary that official relations between the United States and a particular country be hostile in order for Muslims in that country to be poorly disposed to America. A strong sense of Muslim solidarity—called *ummah*—causes Muslims in Turkey or Indonesia to feel keenly and somewhat personally the perceived injustices of the policies of United States in the Israeli-Palestinian conflict. This solidarity has been facilitated in recent years by what has become known as "the al-Jazeera effect," the simultaneous broadcasting of images and interpretations of Middle East conflict to Muslim viewers throughout the world. However, *ummah* could not be promoted through the satellite broadcasts of al-Jazeera in the absence of a cultural predisposition toward a kind of solidarity that enables Muslim viewers—whether in Jakarta or Dearborn—to interpret American policies in the Middle East as hostile toward Muslims in general, not merely toward Palestinians or a particular regime.

All in all, however, the hypothesis that state-to-state hostility equals greater anti-Americanism is not particularly robust. In many ways, the populations of such countries as Jordan, Indonesia, and Turkey appear to be no more anti-American, and perhaps even more admiring of many aspects of America, than the populations of some of the United States' traditional allies, including France, Germany, and Belgium. The strong military support that the United States has provided to South Korea for decades has not prevented a sharp drop in the level of favorable affect toward America among Koreans in recent years. Some survey evidence suggests that even Iranians, whose official relations with the United States have been icy since the end of the 1970s, are not overwhelmingly anti-American, despite persistent negative official portrayals of "the Great Satan" (Clawson 2004).

"WHAT THEY THINK ABOUT US SAYS MORE ABOUT THEM THAN IT DOES ABOUT US"

Although much of the post-9/11 analysis of foreign sentiments toward and perceptions of the United States has focused on American accountability—its policies, values, and actions abroad—some analysts have turned their attention to those who hold these sentiments and perceptions. They have asked the question, "What is it about *them* that leads these populations or opinion leaders—or both—to view us as they do?" In fact, explanations that emphasize the cultural and psychological traits and material interests of the beholder are not new. Paul Hollander's masterful account of anti-Americanism, domestic and foreign, is based on the premise that this phenomenon has considerably more to do with characteristics of opinion leaders than it does with the objective reality of America. Andrei Markovits has recently offered a penetrating examination of the anti-Americanism of the European intelligentsia that demonstrates how it functions similarly to other prejudices.

This explanation of how others see America may be expressed as a formal hypothesis: *If a country's identity, self-image, or perception of its status in the world is dependent upon its image of America, then that country's population is more likely to have intense feelings toward the United States.* This hypothesis says nothing, however, about whether these sentiments will be positive or negative. Although intense feelings toward the United States are often associated with high levels of disapproval, as occurred in many countries leading up to and after the 2003 invasion of Iraq, high intensity is not necessarily associated with anti-Americanism. For example, foreign sympathy and positive feelings toward the United States spiked in the immediate aftermath of 9/11. Moreover, in English Canada, where a preoccupation with the United States has long been a distinguishing feature of the culture, intense feelings do not necessarily carry a negative affect. Canadians have long exhibited a mixture of feelings toward their American neighbors, some being anti-American, others being pro-American, and most being ambivalent.

Clearly, strong feelings alone do not account for anti-Americanism. Therefore, in order to understand anti-American sentiments, our hypothesis needs to be refined: *If a population's self image is improved as a result of a negative impression of the United States, anti-Americanism will be greater. Similarly, if the status, prestige, and material aspirations of a country's opinion leaders are advanced by a negative image of the United States, then they are more likely to generate and disseminate anti-American interpretations and images.*

A good deal of empirical evidence supports this hypothesis. Let us consider four cases: Russia, France, Canada, and Islamists (or Muslim extremists).

Russia

No one has studied contemporary Russian attitudes toward America more closely than Vladimir Shlapentokh, a professor at Michigan State University. Shlapentokh argues that in post-Soviet Russia, a significant gap has opened

between the masses and elites when it comes to their beliefs about and feelings toward America. Based on a number of opinion surveys, he notes that
a clear majority of Russians report having an overall positive stance toward
America. Despite being inclined to view American culture and business
practices negatively, Russians tend to admire specific features of life in
America as they perceive it, and believe that when it comes to honesty and
fairness, the American electoral and legal systems are superior to their own
(Shlapentokh 2001, 18).

Russian elites, however, view America quite differently. They tend to be
strongly anti-American, a generalization that cuts across ideological lines.
One Russian commentator goes so far as to characterize the stance of the
elites as "pathological anti-Americanism" (cited in Shlapentokh 2001, 20).
Shlapentokh's explanation for the Russian elite's hostility toward America is
as follows:

> The members of the ruling class want to rationalize their failure to
> build a "normal" liberal society, particularly in light of the success of
> other post-Communist countries.... This class also wants to rational-
> ize its deep involvement in corruption and criminal activities, and per-
> suade themselves and the world that they are "normal people" living
> in a "normal society." To meet these ideological and psychological
> goals, Russian elites have developed various anti-Western images. (19)

To this, Shlapentokh adds,

> Elites must maintain negative attitudes toward the West to pursue a
> career in the political and cultural establishments in Russia. Those who
> proclaim friendly attitudes toward the United States have no chance for
> a career in Moscow. (20)

Anti-Americanism, Shlapentokh argues, enables post-Soviet Russian
elites to feel better about themselves and their society by attributing to
America traits and motives that put their erstwhile cold war rival in an
unfavorable light. Shlapentokh focuses on the *functional role* that anti-
Americanism plays in contemporary Russia, a role that need not have much
connection to the reality of America and that, in fact, requires that a distorted image be constructed. Interestingly, distorted images of America

probably also served a functional role during the cold war among Soviet dissidents, whose oppressed and even dangerous condition likely led them to a certain degree of romanticizing about the United States. Now that Russian intellectuals and other elites are free from the sort of persecution that squelched public dissent during the Soviet era, the West—particularly the United States—appears less a beacon than a symbol of reproach for the problems that afflict post-Communist Russia. Withdrawal into a negative image of America—disparaging its features and blaming it for at least some of Russia's ills—is embraced by most Russian elites.

France

In recent years, no Western society has been more anti-American than France, and no democracy's elites have been more deeply and persistently critical of American values, institutions, actions, and policies than the French. The intensity of these feelings has increased since the 2000 election of George W. Bush and especially since the invasion of Iraq, but this is merely a spike in a more general and long-standing pattern of anti-Americanism whose explanation requires an understanding of the place that America occupies in the imagination of most of France's elites. Andrei Markovits uses the term *ressentiment*—the French word for resentment, but with connotations of a deeper, more passionate emotion—to character-ize the roots of the hostility that French elites have long expressed toward the United States. He places the emphasis, therefore, on the holders of the hostile sentiments rather than their object.

It is often said by the French themselves that they are obsessed with America. Of course, the Brits often say the same thing about themselves, and anyone who has ever studied Canada or spent some time observing life there knows it to be true of Canadians as well. When Tocqueville wrote, "Although I very rarely spoke of France in my book, I did not write one page of it without having her, so to speak, before my eyes," he was setting a course that would be followed by subsequent generations of French intel-lectuals. Although Tocqueville's magisterial *Democracy in America* does not want for empirical observation and description, what America's most famous foreign observer set out to do was explain to his fellow Frenchmen what America meant for human history. To use a distinction that Markovits employs in his analysis of European anti-Americanism, Tocqueville was more interested in what America *was* than what it *did*: its being rather than its actions.

This distinction is necessary in order to understand the roots of the anti-Americanism of French elites. It is not so much the policies of the United States government or the actions of Americans abroad that the French elites object to, although these have often come in for passionate criticism. Rather, it has been what America represents in their eyes: naiveté, low culture, a tendency to understand the world in simplistic terms, barbarity, religious fundamentalism, hypocrisy, vulgar materialism, and ignorance and insensitivity when it comes to the rest of the world. These are some of the tropes that routinely inform French commentary on America. Jean Baudrillard—no fan of America—sees clearly that what French elites chiefly resent is that America is, in fact, the authentic face of modernity, warts and all. It is far too simple to attribute French resentment and anti-Americanism to France's diminished stature in the world; in other words, to interpret them as products of envy. Although envy may be an aspect of French anti-Americanism, it is far from being the key to the hostility and disdain that characterize French opinion leaders. French elites recognize, quite correctly, that America represents a model of society quite different from theirs, and that maintaining the prestige and validity of their own preferred system depends on repudiating and denigrating that of the United States.

The construction of a European identity centered around the institutions of the European Union (EU), a project that is embraced by most French opinion leaders, requires a measure of hostility toward America and is built on a foundation of anti-Americanism. "History teaches us," says Markovits, "that *any* entity—certainly in its developing stages—only attains consciousness and self-awareness by defining itself in opposition to another entity" (2003). Anti-Americanism has performed this function for French elites, and Western European elites more generally, in recent years. Markovits writes, "With the entity of Europe now being on the agenda, anti-Americanism may well serve as a useful coagulating function for the establishment of this new entity, and become a potent political force on the mass level way beyond the elites' [longstanding] antipathy and *réssentiment*." The meaning that French elites ascribe to America becomes the measure against which they define what they maintain is a more humane, civilized, and just alternative.

Canada

No serious discussion of a distinctive Canadian identity in English-speaking Canada (French Canada being an entirely separate matter) can ignore the crucial role that anti-Americanism has played in its construction and maintenance. Sociologist and longtime student of Canada-US differences Seymour Martin Lipset points out that, like the United States, English Canada was born out of the American Revolution. Two societies would emerge from that war: the United States, which supported the revolution and thereafter defined itself in terms of the liberal and republican values in whose name the break from Britain was made; and Canada, the country of the counter-revolution, to which thousands of colonists immigrated after the defeat of British forces. In turning their backs on the new independent republic to the south, these proto-Canadians (Canada would not achieve semi-independence until 1867) faced a dilemma. They were not significantly different from their American cousins in terms of language, ethnicity, or religion, and their core values were generally similar to those of citizens in Massachusetts and New York, but they had made the decision to remain loyal to the British crown. To construct a narrative that would explain their refusal to join Americans in an independent republic under a democratic constitution, they needed more than this loyalty alone. From this need was born the myth of difference: a tendency to exaggerate cultural and other differences separating English Canada from the United States. Criticism of traits attributed to Americans—their values, behaviors, and institutions—combined with an insistence on the moral superiority of Canada have always been crucial to English Canada's narrative of distinctiveness.

No national identity is as tied to an image of America as that of English Canada. Confronted with the overwhelming economic and cultural power of the United States, a country with which they share a border, a language, and much culture and history, English Canadian elites have understood that their status, prestige, and prospects require various forms of defense against American competition. For most of the country's history, the Canadian capitalist class was staunchly protectionist, supporting high tariffs and restrictions on foreign (mainly American) investment in such sectors of the economy as banking, transportation, and communication. Canadian cultural elites have relied on the state to subsidize their livelihoods and ensure that a supply of Canadian-made culture exists. State elites have often seen in protectionist measures the necessary means to protect their authority and relevance. In making the case for a publicly owned broadcasting system, Robert Aird, one of its architects, summed up this need as "the state or the United States." This phrase has been the mantra of English Canadian nationalists ever since. Some of these nationalists themselves have occasionally lamented the degree to which the identity of English Canada has been so dependent on state intervention.

When a case is being made for protecting or promoting some aspect of English Canadian culture, identity, or independence, a negative image of the United States is almost invariably invoked. Hostility toward America and its perceived attributes serves two important functions: It distinguishes Canada from its southern neighbor and, at the same time, validates the role and prestige of the nationalist elites, who are largely dependent on a life-support system of state subsidies, public agencies, and other forms of protection. But although anti-Americanism is deeply ingrained in Canadian society—produced and reproduced by successive generations of opinion leaders—it is much less intense today, and there is nowhere near the degree of anti-American consensus that one finds among the opinion-shaping classes in such countries as France and Germany.

Alongside the nationalist defenders of Canadian identity, culture, and institutions are the elites whose stance toward the United States is considerably friendlier. Most prominent among them are the representatives of industries who believe that their business prospects would be improved, rather than threatened, by more openness and integration with the American economy. They achieved major victories with the 1989 Canada-US Free Trade Agreement, and then again with NAFTA in 1993. The interests of industry have found allies in some segments of the opinion-shaping classes of English Canada, such as the Fraser Institute, a market-oriented think tank, and the CanWest Global Communications Corporation, whose newspapers tend to be more sympathetic to the United States than much of the Canadian mass media. Some prominent journalists and public intellectuals can also be counted on to criticize the motives and arguments of their anti-American colleagues. Canadians may be the oldest and most practiced anti-Americans, but their opinion leaders have always been divided in their stance toward the United States, and the sentiments of the general population have never been as intense as those of the nationalists who claim to speak on their behalf.

Muslim Extremists

From the time of the Iranian Revolution to Osama bin Laden and al Qaeda, the United States has been portrayed by some Muslims as "the Great Satan." Although many Muslims may abhor what they see as moral laxity in the West and America's favoritism toward Israel in the conflict with the Palestinians, the perception of the United States as the embodiment of evil does not appear to be shared by the majority of the world's Muslims. It is, however, expressed by some militant Muslims and by some influential leaders in parts of the Muslim community in countries throughout the world.

The masterminds behind the attacks of 9/11 and those who carried them out clearly believed that America represented something worse than a morally sick society with a penchant for taking sides against Muslim countries. In Bin Laden's 1998 interview with ABC reporter John Miller on *Frontline*, the al Qaeda leader emphasized his view that all Muslims have a duty to wage war against the United States and kill American soldiers and civilians, whose government "is leading the country towards hell." Bin Laden is the best-known but far from the only Muslim leader to characterize America as the embodiment of evil, a satanic force in world affairs whose values and actions threaten Muslims wherever they may be. Many prominent Muslim clerics and intellectuals have made similar arguments, going back a half-century.

Casting the United States as "the Great Satan" has proved an influential tool for mobilizing public opinion in parts of the Muslim world, supporting the legitimacy of particular regimes such as Iran's, and inspiring personal motivation for those who believe martyrdom is the means to combat the evil that they think America represents. However, the less extreme portrayal of the United States as morally corrupt, unduly influenced by Jews, and implacably opposed the Islamic world has greater resonance among the majority of Muslims. Not all spokespersons for Islamic fundamentalism characterize America as "the Great Satan." But it *is* fair to say that virtually all of them accept this less-extreme portrayal of America and its government.

Even if we accept that part of the explanation for portraying America as evil is rooted in the objective reality of American society and the actions of its government abroad, the picture is grotesquely exaggerated, and, moreover, not fully embraced by the mass public in the Muslim world (see the analysis of Muslim ambivalence toward America in chapter 3). To fully explain the image of America projected by Islamic fundamentalist leaders, it is necessary to understand how their own status, prestige, and legitimacy require that they vilify, if not demonize, America. Islam scholar Bernard Lewis articulates the best known of such functional explanations. He has long argued that the rise of militant and fundamentalist Islam in the last half-century is largely due to resentment over the undeniable decline of Islam's stature in the contemporary world and the effort to locate the source of this deterioration in the actions and values of the West. As the obvious embodiment of what the West represents, the United States has been the chief target of this anger and resentment. "Islamic fundamentalism," Lewis writes, "has given an aim and a form to the otherwise aimless and formless resentment and anger of the Muslim masses at the forces [of modernity] that have devalued their traditional values and loyalties and, in the final analysis, robbed them of their beliefs, their aspirations, their dignity, and to an increasing extent their livelihood" (Lewis 1990). In his best-selling book *What Went Wrong* (2002), Lewis makes clear that he does not believe there is anything inherent in Islam's history and the Muslim religious tradition that explains the decline in the prestige and influence of Islam over the last few centuries. But for a number of reasons, the Muslim world failed to adapt to modernity. Faced with what was seen as a humiliating decline in its status and influence in the world, and increasing competition from non-Muslim values and ways at home, elites in much of the Muslim world have reacted with outrage, revulsion against the West, and, in some Muslim societies, a reassertion of what are ostensibly the true ways and values of the faithful.

This outrage and revulsion, this resentment stemming from feelings of humiliation and threat to Muslim values, could not have influenced the ideas and actions of the masses as widely and deeply as it appears to have without the encouragement of the elites, whose legitimacy and influence in their own countries depended on channeling this bitterness into blame and anti-Americanism. It bears repeating that many of what the Muslim world perceives to be the institutions and accomplishments of America are admired by much of the general public. But alongside this admiration in societies like Jordan, Turkey, Egypt, and even Iran (Clawson 2004) exists undeniable hostility toward the United States—hostility that predates the Bush administration and the invasion of Iraq. The so-called "al-Jazeera effect" has almost certainly widened the scope and deepened the intensity of this hostility. But

BOX 6.2   A Message from "New Europe"?

The real bond between the US and Europe is the values we share: democracy, individual freedom, human rights, and the rule of law. These values crossed the Atlantic with those who sailed from Europe to help create the United States of America. Today they are under greater threat than ever.

The attacks of September 11 showed just how far terrorists—the enemies of our common values—are prepared to go to destroy them. Those outrages were an attack on all of us. In standing firm in defense of these principles, the governments and people of the US and Europe have amply demonstrated the strength of their convictions. Today more than ever, the trans-Atlantic bond is a guarantee of our freedom. We in Europe have a relationship with the US that has stood the test of time. Thanks in large part to American bravery, generosity, and farsightedness, Europe was set free from the two forms of tyranny that devastated our continent in the twentieth century: Nazism and Communism. Thanks, too, to the continued cooperation between Europe and the US we have managed to guarantee peace and freedom on our continent. The trans-Atlantic relationship must not become a casualty of the current Iraqi regime's persistent attempts to threaten world security.

Source: From a joint statement by the prime ministers of Denmark, Hungary, Italy, Poland, Portugal, Spain, and the UK, and the president of the Czech Republic, issued on January 30, 2003, during the lead-up to the war in Iraq.

even before al-Jazeera began to inflame passions and contribute to an aggrieved sense of *ummah*, a widespread feeling of injustice pervaded the Muslim world, given voice and fueled by Muslim opinion leaders.

Without glossing over or diminishing the reality that American actions have caused some hostility among the elites and the masses in the Muslim world, it would require a rather closed mind to deny that Muslim elites have frequently used anti-Americanism to scapegoat the United States—often in tandem with Israel or "the Jews"—for their own internal problems. Even Edward Said, the implacable a critic of American policy toward the Arab world, would regularly acknowledge that Arab and Muslim leaders and intellectuals occasionally use anti-Americanism as a cover for problems of their own making. Hazen Saglujeh, who writes for the Arabic newspaper *al-Hayat* in London, says much the same thing. "Arab intellectuals," he writes, "who ought to encourage change, have largely failed in that role. For the most part, they did not detach themselves from the tribal tradition of defending 'our' causes in the face of the 'enemy.' Their priority has not been to criticize the incredible shortcomings that they live with…. Thus they help stereotype themselves before being stereotyped by any enemy" (Saglujeh 2001, 55).

Of course, the temptation to portray America in false or exaggerated colors, assigning blame and motives even in circumstances where this is patently unreasonable, may be understandable. When the Ayandeh Institute in Iran published the results of a 2002 poll showing that 74 per cent of Iranians favored resumption of relations with the United States and almost half expressed the view that US policies toward Iran were "to some extent correct," the pollsters were sentenced to lengthy jail terms (Ashouri 2003, 2). Fear of the potential consequences of expressing views that might be interpreted as critical of the political or clerical authorities may have at least as powerful an influence on what opinion leaders write and say as the desire for position and prestige.

"A COMMON ENEMY PROMOTES BONDS OF SYMPATHY AND SOLIDARITY"

Although similar to the hypothesis about government-to-government relations, this explanation of foreign sentiment toward the United States shifts the focus from a country's relationship with America to its perceptions of America's relations with a third party. That party could be another country and its regime, or a movement or organization. Formal hypothesis: *If a population shares with America a perceived external or internal threat, then the likelihood that it will view the United States—its policies and its people—positively is greater.*

Leading up to and during the early stages of the war in Iraq, there appeared to be some evidence to support this hypothesis. Some Eastern European countries, formerly part of the Soviet Union's sphere of influence, appeared to be more supportive of the American-led invasion of Iraq, contributing to what American Secretary of Defense Donald Rumsfeld called a division between "Old" and "New" Europe. Poland, initially an enthusiastic member of "the coalition of the willing" in Iraq, was often held up as the embodiment of this "New Europe." Poles, it was argued, had fresh memories of Communist domination and felt a sense of gratitude toward the United States and sympathy for American leadership in world affairs that "Old Europe," represented by such countries as France and Germany, did not share.

One year after the terrorist attacks of 9/11, the Pew Global Attitudes Project found that popular support for the US-led war on terrorism was indeed higher in some of the countries of formerly Communist Eastern Europe than in Western Europe and Canada (see figure 6.4). Although the gap was not enormous, such countries as Ukraine, Poland, and the Czech Republic showed greater support than the populations of America's traditional NATO allies. This pattern continued in the period leading up to and following the invasion of Iraq. Moreover, the massive anti-war demonstrations and official denunciations in Western Europe were not matched by any comparable opposition in Eastern Europe. Indeed, French Prime Minister Jacques Chirac issued a rebuke to some countries that expressed support for the United States, such as Poland, suggesting that as new members of the EU, they should take their lead in such matters from more senior member-states such as France and Germany.

The divide between "Old" and "New Europe" that Rumsfeld and others have observed does, in fact, exist. But its nature is not as simple as has been suggested. Poles, Czechs, Ukrainians, and the people of other countries formerly under Communist rule are no more likely than Western European populations to express admiration for various aspects of America that have influenced their culture and society or for its accomplishments. But populations and opinion leaders from "New Europe" appear to be more skeptical about relying on the EU for their security and that of the world. This may be because these Eastern European societies have only recently joined the EU and are not accustomed to looking toward Brussels and Strasbourg for leadership. In other words, it may be simply a matter of time before the citizens of Poland and other formerly East Bloc countries internalize a sense of EU citizenship. But in the meantime, they are more likely than people in France, Germany, and Spain to look to the United States for leadership on the economy and international security.

This readiness to look to the United States for leadership may be partially due, as some have suggested, to a still-fresh sense of gratitude for its role in opposing Soviet Communism and its influence in Eastern Europe. The memory of their common enemy contributes to a bond of sympathy with America. But memories, of course, grow dimmer with the passage of time. Nonetheless, it is hard to imagine a Polish foreign minister taking the American government to task in the testy and public way that Germany's Joschka Fischer did in the lead up to the invasion of Iraq, when he stated

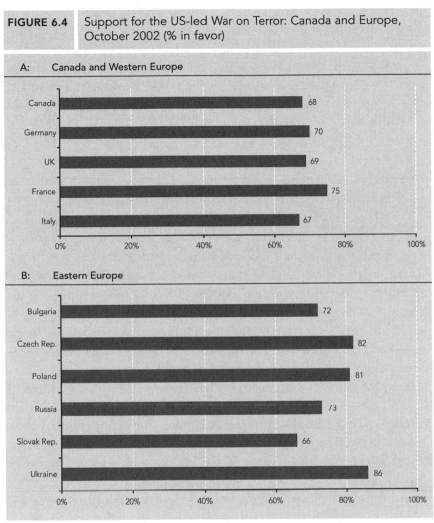

FIGURE 6.4 Support for the US-led War on Terror: Canada and Europe, October 2002 (% in favor)

A: Canada and Western Europe

B: Eastern Europe

Source: Adapted from The Pew Center for the People and the Press, "What the World Thinks in 2002" (November 2002), 58.

that America could no longer count on the goodwill it had earned—by helping defeat Nazism, rebuild Germany, and contain Soviet Communism—to ensure support for America's actions in the world. At the same time, there is no shortage of Polish critics and skeptics of American policies abroad. But unlike such countries as France and Germany, Poland's opinion-leading classes are not overwhelmingly anti-American. Catholic and conservative opinion leaders in Poland, along with a large part of the business community, are sympathetic toward American values and influence in the world. The world view that they embrace and communicate to the Polish people still bears the mark of the cold war. Not only does this mean that they are inclined to see the United States as having been instrumental in their liberation from Communist control and respond with gratitude, they are also more inclined than the opinion-leading classes of Western Europe to understand global conflict in terms of the clash of good and evil. The language and moral architecture of recent American foreign policy, including such terms as "the axis of evil," "evil-doers," "the clash of civilizations," and similar dichotomous characterizations of world conflict, have more traction in a society that, until fairly recently, lived under oppressive rule.

The situation in South Korea also appears to lend some support to the hypothesis that sharing a common enemy with America promotes positive perceptions. For over half a century, the United States has been South Korea's chief military ally in that country's hostile relationship with Communist North Korea. The liberation of Korea from Japanese control at the end of World War II and the subsequent division of the country into North and South, followed by American military interventions on behalf of the South when the North invaded in 1950, established a deep sense of gratitude toward the United States among South Koreans.

In recent years, this appreciation has largely dissipated, particularly among younger South Koreans. But for at least a generation after the Korean War, it remained very strong. A 2003 Gallup-Korea poll found that 75 per cent of respondents in their twenties had an unfavorable view of the United States compared to only 26 per cent of those over the age of 50 (Brooke 2003, 12). Among the younger generation, the sense of gratitude toward America is almost entirely absent and, in fact, has been replaced by a sense of resentment. This is somewhat ironic, given that American culture pervades almost every corner of the younger generation's lifestyle in this very Westernized country. Nevertheless, as Seunglio Sheen observes, "South Korea's younger generation increasingly sees US troops not as guarantors of security but as obstacles to reunification" (Sheen 2003, 96). The older generation can still recall the fear of North Korea, the very real threat it posed, and the official and persistent casting of the North as the enemy. The younger generation, however, has been exposed to former president Kim Dae-jung's "Sunshine" policy of engagement, which humanizes North Koreans as "brothers" and downplays the nuclear threat from the North.

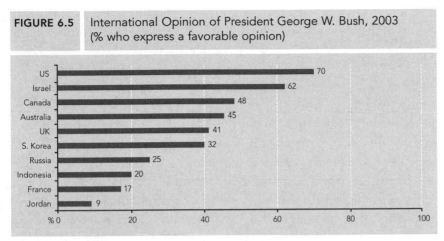

FIGURE 6.5 International Opinion of President George W. Bush, 2003 (% who express a favorable opinion)

US 70
Israel 62
Canada 48
Australia 45
UK 41
S. Korea 32
Russia 25
Indonesia 20
France 17
Jordan 9

% 0   20   40   60   80   100

Source: ICM Research, "What the World Thinks of America," prepared for the BBC (2003).

The memory of American actions in defense of South Korea are not only receding, but are being replaced by a revised historical narrative that largely blames the United States for the partition of Korea and the maintenance of hostility between the North and the South. In addition, the perceived threat posed by North Korea is being overshadowed by South Korea's hope for reunification. As a result, resentment toward the United States has increasingly replaced gratitude among growing numbers of South Koreans. Bonds of sympathy and positive sentiment generated by a common enemy dissolve when that enemy no longer appears particularly threatening, presenting an opportunity for grievances toward the United States to grow and, ultimately, creating a popular wave of anti-Americanism. This is precisely what has transpired in South Korea-US relations.

Finally, Israel is perhaps the best example of the common enemy hypothesis. When elite and popular sentiment toward the United States was in free-fall surrounding the 2003 invasion of Iraq, Israel stood alone as the one democracy in which popular support for America and the war remained high. Israel's famously fractious opinion-leading classes were less overwhelming than the general population in their support of the war and in expressing favorable views of America, but the balance of elite opinion was certainly positive.

The goodwill that so many Israelis feel toward the United States and the generally favorable perceptions they have of America are, of course, due to a number of factors. Israelis sometimes refer to their country as the "fifty-first state," a society that is more American than America itself in many aspects of popular taste and lifestyle. But a large part of the favorable image Israelis have toward the United States must be ascribed to their rather realistic belief that no other country can be counted on to be as loyal an ally and steadfast protector of their security. Prior to the invasion of Iraq, Israelis were far more likely than the populations of other democracies to view Saddam Hussein and Islamist terrorism as real and immediate threats to their country. Predictably, therefore, their support for the American-led war in Iraq and the war on terror was more enthusiastic.

There is, of course, more behind the generally favorable perception of America among Israelis than the sense of a common threat. Ties of people and values, to say nothing of Israel's considerable dependency on state and non-state aid from America, contribute to the positive image that most Israelis have of the United States and its role in the world. But the common threat factor is significant and probably explains why, when President George W. Bush's image throughout most of the world was so low, Israel stood out as the one country in which his approval rating was high—almost as high as it was in the United States!

CHAPTER SEVEN

WHY *the* WORLD'S PERCEPTIONS MATTER

> *Unfortunately, our country has [an image] problem in far too many*
> *parts of the world, a problem we have regrettably gotten into over*
> *many years through both Democrat and Republican administrations,*
> *and a problem that does not lend itself to a quick fix or a simple solu-*
> *tion or a simple plan.*
> —Margaret Tutwiler, State Department, Public Diplomacy, first week
> of February 2004, before House Appropriations subcommittee

This assessment from senior State Department official Margaret Tutwiler, as the American-led occupation of Iraq lurched from bad to worse in early 2004, was only partly correct. The international image of the United States government and its foreign policies had, in fact, deteriorated to an all time low. Negative sentiment and even hatred toward America had spread across more regions of the world than ever before. The roots of this antipathy were, as Tutwiler observed, deeper than the Bush administration's decision to invade Iraq and replace the regime of Saddam Hussein. And the "problem"—from the standpoint of American policy-makers and their goals—could not be solved simply or quickly.

One of the things that is wrong or at least misleading in Tutwiler's cursory diagnosis of America's image problem abroad is its failure to distinguish adequately between how people perceive American foreign policy and their responses to other aspects of America. Another is its failure to acknowledge the volatility in foreign sentiment toward the United States. Tutwiler's testimony went on to convey the impression that fixing the problem of negative foreign perceptions would mainly require better communications to convey the real story of what America stands for—its values, history, and institutions—to hostile populations whose impressions are poisoned by the one-sided and heavily biased portrayals of their local opinion leaders.

Americans cannot assume that "to know us is to love us." Negative perceptions of America are as old as the nation itself and have always coexisted alongside more favorable sentiments. And, as has always been true, the perceptions that others have are only partly based on the actions of the United States and reality of the American experience. It follows from this that America's "image problem" is not and has never been wholly remediable through its own actions.

During a European visit shortly before the 2004 US elections, Rudolph Giuliani remarked that Americans do indeed pay too little attention to the rest of the world and know too little about people and places beyond their borders. But, he added, it is also true that much of the world knows too little that is accurate about America. There is more than a little truth in Giuliani's observation. The amount of misinformation about America can be staggering, and not only in countries that have state-controlled propaganda machines and regimes that are hostile to the United States. As we have seen in previous chapters, the roots and nature of these distorted images vary between countries. Setting the record straight in parts of the world where the image of America is unfairly negative is probably not always possible.

There is, however, some material to work with to improve America's image overseas. Favorable assessments and positive sentiments do exist, even in some of the societies thought to be most virulently and intractably anti-American. As observed in chapter 3, most foreign populations think highly of such aspects of America as its scientific and technological innovation, economic opportunities, and, to a lesser degree, its democratic institutions and respect for freedom of expression. Even American popular culture—film and music in particular—is viewed favorably by majorities in most countries, often the same countries in which majorities also say that they do not think American culture should be emulated. This ambivalence toward America is long-standing and has often been noted. But instead of interpreting it as a problem, which is the usual response, this ambivalence might just as plausibly be viewed as taking some of the edge off anti-Americanism. In other words, the positive capital that the United States has accumulated through the export of those aspects of its culture, lifestyle, and aspirations that tend to be viewed favorably by foreign populations may soften the impact of anti-American sentiment.

If we assume that some considerable degree of foreign anti-Americanism is inevitable—given that it is as old as the European idea of America itself, going back five centuries—the practical question for Americans, their interests abroad, and their government is whether anti-Americanism matters. If it matters, when and why? In posing these questions, I am assuming that the mere fact that they are not loved, or are even hated, is not sufficient reason for Americans to think that they should change other people's perception of them. But when these perceptions affect the interests of the United States and its citizens, their prosperity and security, they matter.

Some will see this as precisely the sort of self-centered view that has fueled anti-Americanism abroad. And, indeed, the insularity from the world outside their borders that has long characterized Americans has almost certainly contributed to the image of them as arrogant and indifferent to the preferences, values, and ways of others. One professor of comparative politics at a prominent American university described to me the approach taken by many of his colleagues: "Other countries are viewed as real estate." If this is the approach taken by many American intellectuals, who can blame the general population for being monumentally ignorant about and indifferent toward the rest of the world, until its reality washes up against their own shores?

At the same time, however, regardless of the intentions behind the United States government's activities abroad and whatever the impact of America's global presence, from movie theaters to military bases, it is inevitable that those actions and consequences, even when they deliver benefits to at least some, will be interpreted as evidence of American perfidy and used to fuel anti-American sentiment. I have been reminded of this fact in conversations with several Western European colleagues concerning the 1999 American military intervention in Kosovo, in response to Slobodan Milosovic's ethnic cleansing of the Muslim population. A popular interpretation of that intervention, which was in fact entered into with considerable reluctance and only after the abject failure of Western European governments and the EU to respond, is that the United States was enthusiastic to defeat a regime that stood in the way of its plan to wipe out opposition to the spread of pro-Western, pro-capitalist regimes throughout Europe. Milosovic's Serbian nationalism stood in the way of this alleged design.

This is, in fact, a ridiculous caricature of the circumstances leading to American involvement in Kosovo. It ignores the fact that most Americans and many of their political leaders vehemently opposed US involvement in the conflict because they did not believe that vital US interests were at stake. Moreover, it attributes to the United States and its leaders a conscious strategy that, at least in this case, was highly improbable. So why is such an interpretation embraced by intelligent people?

The answer, as we have seen from the analysis in chapter 4, is that this interpretation fits the image and understanding of the United States that has been shaped and propagated by national opinion leaders. How else can one make sense of the fact that a former German cabinet minister could write a best-selling book in which he gives succor to the view, already held by a significant share of his country's population, that the CIA and Israel orchestrated the attacks of 9/11 in order to provide a pretext for the war on terror, which would morph into the invasion of Iraq? How else can one explain portrayals of America such as US Media Blues, which was broadcast on one of France's state-owned television stations just before the 2004 US elections and painted the American mass media system—not just Fox and Clear Channel Communications—as complicit in a successful right wing and Republican conspiracy to control the airwaves? How else to explain the fact that most educated young Swedes—along with many other Europeans—are convinced that the United States is the *least* democratic society in the community of North Atlantic democracies? And how to explain the results of surveys that show a large percentage of the population of Muslim societies did not believe that Osama bin Laden and accomplices from Arab countries orchestrated and carried out the attacks of 9/11, while at the same time many were rejoicing in what they perceived as a victorious attack on a vital symbol and citadel of the society Muslims blamed for their humiliation? None of this makes much sense until one stops to recognize that foreign images of America are not rooted solely, and sometimes not even primarily, in the reality of the American condition and American actions. Rudolph Giuliani is doubtless correct when he notes that the flipside of American ignorance of the world beyond its borders is the misinformed—sometimes maliciously—perception of America that is held by many abroad.

Some degree of anti-Americanism in certain parts of the world is inevitable. The love-hate relationship that much of the world, from Canada to Kuwait, has with the United States is long-standing. And, unless America, the "New Rome," were to collapse (a European leftist desire in the 1960s and 1970s that has made a comeback in books like Emmanuel Todd's *After the Empire: The Breakdown of the American Order* and Niall Ferguson's *Colossus: The Price of America's Empire*), this ambivalence is not something that can be eradicated. At the same time, however, American policy-makers should not ignore the very real consequences that follow from negative and seriously misinformed images of their country. While it is pointless to expect that everyone will love the United States, Americans need to mitigate hateful foreign perceptions of them.

The consequences of hate became evident on September 11, 2001. Although anti-Americanism of the sort that has long existed in such countries as Canada, France, and Mexico does not threaten the security of the United States and the lives of its citizens, 9/11 showed that more virulent forms of anti-Americanism can produce devastating results. 9/11 may, without exaggeration, be said to have opened a new chapter in the history of anti-Americanism, one that found Americans and their government unprepared, despite signs (the World Trade Center bombing of 1993, the attacks on the American embassies in Africa, and the attack on the USS *Cole*) that a new, violent strain of the old anti-Americanism was gaining momentum. Although the actual number of people complicit in such attacks was small, it immediately became evident that popular sympathy for their motivations, if not always their means, was considerable across the Muslim world. Terrorism that lacks a base of popular support is far easier to deal with, using intelligence and military means, than that which fueled the attacks leading up to 9/11. Terrorism in the name of goals that are widely admired and targeted at an image of the enemy that resonates with a large population is another matter.

But even when lives at home and abroad are not threatened by anti-Americanism, America's interests may sometimes be jeopardized by unfavorable opinions of and sentiments toward the United States. Since World War II, there has never been a time when the prosperity and security of the United States did not depend on circumstances beyond its borders. Today, however, these interests are so enmeshed that there is no realistic prospect of disentangling America from the world. In practical terms, this means that domestic opinion is not the only opinion that needs to matter for Americans, for those who produce Hollywood's films and those who produce Washington's policies.

This became evident leading up to the 2003 invasion of Iraq, when boycotts of American products appeared a real possibility in markets throughout the Muslim world. Nationalization of American-owned assets without compensation by hostile regimes and foreign laws limiting American investment and attempting to control American economic influence have a long history. But the more recent threat of foreign boycotts has raised the specter of losing foreign markets upon which American prosperity partly depends.

The recent emergence of "Muslim colas" as competitors to Atlanta-based Coca-Cola, the world's most recognized product brand, is perhaps the most visible case of this threat. In 2002, French Muslim businessman Tawfiq Mathlouthi launched Mecca-Cola on the French market. This was followed in 2003 by Qibla-Cola on the British market, under the leadership of British Muslim entrepreneur Zafer Iqbal. In both cases, the marketing of the new brand was explicitly political, stressing that the rejection of Coca-Cola in favor of the Islamic equivalent was both a gesture of *ummah* and a consumer's vote against the international might of America. While the potential losses to Coca-Cola sales in these countries are not negligible—Britain has a Muslim population of about 2 million and France about 4 million—they are far from catastrophic. More serious is the possibility of losses in developing markets such as Pakistan and Indonesia, where not only are current sales significant, but potential exists for massive growth. As Ahmet Bozer, Coca-Cola's president for the Eurasia and Middle East regions, observes, "Obviously, in some markets we acknowledge that our sales have been impacted to some extent ... but boycotts really hurt the local economy.... When the boycott takes effect then [the thousands of local people we employ, directly and indirectly] may be put out of jobs" (BBC 2004). This argument may, however, prove to be rather ineffective against what some have described as the possibility of a boycott "jihad" against American multinationals.

Coca-Cola, McDonald's, Hollywood, Nike, and Microsoft are all elements of the American "brand" that are consumed abroad. Their actions sometimes spur anti-Americanism, as when the global expansion of McDonald's symbolizes American assault to local cultures and producers.

But these outposts of corporate America may further become targets of overseas violence, boycotts, or government measures to restrict their markets when the climate of anti-Americanism captures all highly visible symbols of America in its sweep. Business for Diplomatic Action (BDA), created in 2003 by advertising CEO Keith Reinhard, is a corporate NGO that aims to improve America's image abroad in order to reduce precisely these sorts of risks to US businesses who invest, sell, and produce abroad. "The alarming rise in anti-American sentiment," observes BDA, "represents a looming crisis for US businesses, especially for US brands marketed abroad" (2004). The same globalization that creates opportunities for American investment, sales, and production abroad also creates new and unprecedented vulnerabilities. Some of these vulnerabilities may be caused, or at least exploited, by anti-American popular sentiment in foreign markets. To put this a bit differently, the prospects for *particular* American brands marketed abroad may be affected by the condition of *the* American brand.

Through its public diplomacy programs, the US State Department attempts to market "Brand America." The challenge can be daunting, as the State Department discovered in 2002 when it ran its Shared Values campaign in Muslim television markets. The ads featured ordinary Muslim Americans living their faith in the United States and finding acceptance and personal warmth from their non-Muslim neighbors. They were not well received by the Muslim communities they targeted. Part of the problem appeared to be that the ads were in English, which probably suggested cultural assimilation to Muslims abroad rather than the intended message of tolerance toward Muslim immigrants in the US. But it also seems that the ads were judged in large measure on the basis of their source. The Shared Values campaign failed to overcome the skepticism of viewers who were disposed to see the ads as propaganda from a country whose government was hostile to their culture and interests.

In addition to the self-interested reasons why Americans and their government should be concerned about how others view them, there is another compelling explanation for why the world's perceptions matter—not simply for Americans but for people throughout the world. One of the paradoxes of our times is that even though globalization has led to a world economy that is increasingly interdependent, political and military power are about as concentrated today as they have been since the Roman Empire. The end of the cold war has left the United States as a sort of global colossus, with a defense budget as large as the combined budgets of the next top-twenty military spenders, and with unmatched political weight in virtually all corners of the world. Even if we imagine a future in which China catches up to or even surpasses the United States in economic power, unless this is accompanied by some major revolution in Chinese politics, it is hard to imagine China acquiring the political and cultural prestige of the United States. Some believe that the EU, with a population greater than that of the United States, has the potential to rival America's political influence in the world. But enormous obstacles still prevent Europe from speaking and acting as one. Moreover, to the extent that international leverage is linked to the ability to put troops on the ground, planes in the air, and enforce agreements with might, the EU faces what could be the insurmountable obstacle of widespread pacifist sentiment in many of its leading countries.

But one of the lessons of recent history is that even the "New Rome" cannot bestride the world without wobbling and even tripping from time to time. Unmatched military power combined with unparalleled economic and cultural influence and the prestige of "Brand America" were not enough to deliver the quick and neat achievement of the Bush administration's goals in Iraq. Regime change in Iraq, followed by steps toward democratization, would likely have been achieved with less loss of life if the American-led coalition had included more of the world's major democracies in addition to the United Kingdom, and if their participation had included significant troops and money. For various reasons, this did not happen, and the United States found itself bearing 90 per cent of the costs of the war in Iraq and suffering about 90 per cent of the coalition casualties. To add insult to injury, the failure to achieve a coalition that had more political credibility than the Anglo-American partnership made it fairly easy for critics to level charges of unilateralism and portray the United States as an imperial aggressor bent on making the world safe for American owners of gas-guzzling SUVs. Had either France, Germany, or Russia defected from the United Nations Security Council's majority against military intervention in Iraq, foreign perception of the ensuing invasion and its aftermath might well have been quite different.

Foreign public opinion does matter. While it is true, as we heard during the 2004 US presidential election campaign, that there are no votes in Leipzig, this should not be interpreted as a reason for complacency or indifference toward the views and preferences of other nations. The United

States cannot do without the support of other democracies and hope to maintain any semblance of leadership and credibility in international affairs. It is not realistic to expect that this support will always be forth-coming. Moreover, some would argue that the gap between American values and those of other Western democracies is widening, and therefore it is less likely that concordance can be reached on the best way to deal with the trouble spots of the world. Nevertheless, the indifference toward the opinions of populations whose shared history, values, and institutions should make them natural friends of America must eventually lead to a decline in the moral authority of America's policies and actions abroad. If America is to be an empire of democratic values, as Michael Ignatieff and others argue it can and should be, and not an old-style empire of oppression, as so many of its critics charge it has become, the voices of other societies, especially those most likely to share its aspirations and ideals, cannot be ignored.

References

All Bookstores. 2004. <http://www.allbookstores.com/bestsellers/bestof2002>. Accessed April 22, 2004.

Almond, Gabriel and Sidney Verba. 1963. *The Civic Culture: Political Attitudes and Democracy in Five Nations*. Princeton, NJ: Princeton University Press.

Arendt, Hannah. n.d. "Dream and Nightmare," in *Arendt: Essays in Understanding 1930-1954*, ed. Jerome Kohn. 1994. New York: Harcourt, Brace and Co.

Ashouri, Nazgol. 2003. "Polling in Iran: Surprising Questions." *Policy Watch* no.757. Washington Institute for Near East Policy, May 14.

The Atlantic. 2004. "The Passion of the Arab World." July-August.

Baudrillard, Jean. 1988. *America*. New York: Verso.

BBC (British Broadcasting Corporation). 2003. *What the World Thinks of America*. Broadcast on CBC (Canadian Broadcasting Corporation), June 17.

BBC (British Broadcasting Corporation). 2004. *Message in a Bottle*. Broadcast CBC's *The Passionate Eye*, March 29.

BBC/ICM (British Broadcasting Corporation/ICM Research). 2003. "What the World Thinks of America." Survey conducted by ICM for BBC. <http://www.icmresearch.co.uk/reviews/2003/bbc-wtwta-june-2003_htm>.

Beauvoir, Simone de. 1948. *America Day by Day*. (Reprint 1999. trans. Carol Cosman. Berkeley: University of California Press.)

Brooke, James. 2003. "When Americans Thwart Lovesick Koreans." *New York Times*. October 12, section 4.

Brooks, Stephen. 2002. *America through Foreign Eyes: Classic Interpretations of American Political Life*. Toronto: Oxford University Press.

Bryce, James. 1888. *The American Commonwealth*. (Reprint 1959. New York: G.P. Putnam's Sons.)

Buchanan, William and Hadley Cantril. 1953. *How Nations See Each Other: A Study in Public Opinion*. Urbana, Il: University of Illinois Press.

Business for Diplomatic Action .2004. <http://www.businessfordiplomatic action.org>.

CBC (Canadian Broadcasting Corporation). 1999. *Our Neighbours, Ourselves*. Documentary broadcast on *The Journal*.

Chiozza, Giacomo. 2004. Love and Hate: Anti-Americanism and the American World Order. Paper presented at the University of Michigan, November 16.

Christian Science Monitor. 2002. "International Bestsellers: What's Being Read around the World." February 7.

Clawson, Patrick. 2004. "The Paradox of Anti-Americanism in Iran." <http://meria.idc.ac.il/journal/ 2004/issue1/clawson.pdf>.

Cohen, Andrew. 2000. "Planet America." A five-part series in *The Globe and Mail*, October 14–18.

Crèvecoeur, St. Jean de and J. Hector. 1782. *Letters from an American Farmer*. London: T. Davies.

La Croix. 2000. "Les Américains et nous." A series published each Tuesday from September 26 to December 19.

Debray, Regis. 2002. *L'Edit de Caracalla ou plaidoyer pour des Etats-Unis d'Occident*. Paris: Editions Fayard.

——. 2003. "Nous sommes tous américains," *Harper's*, May 13–17.

Dodge, Martin and Rob Kitchin. 2000. *Mapping Cyberspace*. London: Routledge.

Duhamel, Georges. 1930. *Amérique: scenes de la vie future*. Paris: Editions Fayard.

The Economist. 2005. "The World through Their Eyes." February 24:25.

Evans, J. Martin. 1979. *America: The View from Europe*. Stanford: Stanford Alumni Association.

Ferrero, Guglielmo. 1913. "The Riddle of America." *The Atlantic*. November.

Fleeson, Lucinda. 2004. "Bureau of Missing Bureaus." *American Journalism Review*, February.

Fo, Darius. 2001. Email message first cited in print in *The New York Times*, September 22.

France-Amerique. 2004. "L'anti-Américanisme en débat." <http:// www.france-amerique.com/infos/ dossier/Anti-americanisme/ AntiUS1.htm>. Accessed October 16, 2004.

Frontline. 1998. John Miller's interview with Osama bin Laden. May. <http://www.pbs.org/wgbh/pages/ frontline/shows/binladen/who/ miller.html>.

Fulford, Robert. 2003. "Bashing the US Makes Us Feel Good All Over." *National Post*, September 22.

Granatstein, J.L. 1997. *Yankee Go Home! Canadians and Anti-Americanism*. Toronto: Harper Collins.

Granta. 2002. *What We Think of America*. New York: Granta Publications. Issue 77 (Spring).

Gurowski, Adam de. 1857. "America and Europe." *Putnam's Monthly*. Vol. 9, issue 54.

Hertoghe, Alain. 2003. *La guerre à outrances*. Paris: Calmann-Lévy.

Hollander, Paul. 1992. *Anti-Americanism*. New York: Oxford University Press.

Ignatieff, Michael. 2003. "The Burden." *New York Times Magazine*, January 5.

Inglehart, Ronald and Miguel Basánez et al. eds. 2004. *Human Values and Beliefs: A Cross Cultural Sourcebook*. Based on the 1999–2002 World Values Surveys. Mexico: Siglo Veintiuno Editores.

Inglehart, Ronald and Pippa Norris. 2003. "The True Clash of Civilizations." *Foreign Policy*, March–April.

Joffe, Josef. 2001. "Who's Afraid of Mr. Big?" *The National Interest*. (Summer.)

Kagan, Robert. 2002. "Power and Weakness." *Policy Review*. <http://www.policyreview.org/JUN02/kagan.html>.

Laski, Harold. 1948. *The American Democracy*. New York: Viking Press.

Lawrence, D.H. 1923. "The Evening Land." Published in *Birds, Beast, and Flowers*. London: Cresset Press.

Lewis, Bernard. 1990. "The Roots of Muslim Rage." *The Atlantic*, September. Vol. 266, no.3. <http://www.theatlantic.com/issues/90sep/rage.htm>.

———. 2002. *What Went Wrong? The Clash Between Islam and Modernity in the Middle East*. New York: Oxford University Press.

Lindaman, Dana and Kyle Ward. 2004. *History Lessons: How Textbooks from around the World Portray US History*. New York: New Press.

Lippman, Walter. 1922. *Public Opinion*. New York: Harcourt, Brace and Co.

Marianne. 2004. "Le vrai histoire de la liberation." no. 379, July 24–30.

Markovits, Andrei. 2003. European Anti-Americanism: Past and Present of a Pedigreed Prejudice. Paper delivered at the University of Michigan, September 24.

Moisi, Dominique. 2001. "L'Amérique: ange ou démon?" *Le Nouvel Observateur*. December 13.

Le Monde. 2000. "Voyage au coeur de l'empire." Special supplement, October 20.

Moyer, Bill. 1994. *Consuming Images*. Part of a four-episode series entitled *The Public Mind*. Broadcast on PBS (Public Broadcasting System). Princeton NJ: Films for the Humanities.

National Geographic-Roper. 2002. Global Geographic Literacy Survey. November. <http://geosurvey.nationalgeographic.com/geosurvey/>.

National Public Radio (NPR). 2004. "The Power of Images." Broadcast on All Things Considered, May 10.

Nouvel Observateur. 2002. "L'Amérique, ange ou demon?" December 13.

——. 2004. "L'Amérique qu'on aime." January 22.

O'Rourke, P.J. 2004. "Adult-Male-Elephant Diplomacy." The Atlantic. September.

Pamuk, Orhan. 2001. "The Anger of the Damned." The New York Review of Books, November 15.

Pauwels, Jacques. 2002. The Myth of the Good War: America in the Second World War. Toronto: James Lorimer.

Pew Center for the People and the Press. 2002a. Global Attitudes Project. December 4.

——. 2002b. Biennial News Consumption Survey. June 9.

——. 2003. "War with Iraq Further Divides Global Publics." June 3.

——. 2004. "A Year after Iraq War: Mistrust of America in Europe Ever Higher, Muslim Anger Persists." March 16.

Pintak, Lawrence. 2003. Seeds of Hate: How America's Flawed Middle East Policy Ignited the Jihad. London: Pluto Press.

Revel, Jean-François. 2002. L'Obsession anti-américaine: son fonctionnement, ses causes, ses inconsequences. Paris: Plon.

Roger, Philippe. 2002. L'Ennemi américain: genealogie de l'anti-américainisme francais. Paris: Seuil.

Ross, George. 1991. "French Intellectuals from Sartre to Soft Ideology. " Quoted in Intellectuals and Politics. Charles Lemert, ed. Newbury Park, CA: Sage.

RTBF (Régie de télévision de Belgique français). 2003. "Edition spéciale: Iraq." March 26.

Saglujeh, Hazen. 2001. "It's Not All America's Fault." Time. October 15.

Sardar, Ziauddin and Merryl Wyn Davies. 2002. Why Do People Hate America? London: Icon Books.

Scruton, Roger. 2002a. The West and the Rest: Globalization and the Terrorism Threat. London: ISI Books.

Scruton, Roger. 2002b. "The New Imperium," National Review Online. <http://www.national review.com>. September 26.

Sheen, Seunglio. 2003. "Grudging Partner: South Korea." Asian Affairs. (Summer) 30:2.

Shlapentokh, Vladimir. 2001. "Russian Attitudes toward America: A split between the Ruling Class and the Masses." World Affairs. (Summer) vol. 164, no. 1.

Solzhenitsyn, Aleksandr. 1978. "A World Split Apart." Commencement address at Harvard University, June 8.

The State of the News Media. 2004. Annual Report on American Journalism. <http://www.stateofthemedia.org>.

Steinbeck, John. 1966. "Americans and the World." (Reprinted in 2003 in *America and Americans*. New York: Penguin Books.)

Tocqueville, Alexis de. 1835. *Democracy in America Vol. I.* (Reprint 1994. Toronto: Alfred A. Knopf.)

Tocqueville, Alexis de. 1840. *Democracy in America Vol. II.* (Reprint 1994. Toronto: Alfred A. Knopf.)

Von Bulow, Andreas. 2003. *Die CIA und der 11 September*. Munich: Piper.

Waterbury, John. 2003. "Hate Your Policies, Love Your Institutions," *Foreign Affairs*, January-February.

Index